CONTENTS

Acknowledgements 9
Introduction 11

Chapter 1   In the Beginning: Duplicitous Politics   15
Chapter 2   Haphazard Recordkeeping   22
Chapter 3   "A Pretty Safe Place of Retreat for Bears and Other Wild Animals"   29
Chapter 4   Opening Up "New Country": The Glastenbury Plank Road   38
Chapter 5   Charcoal Fueled Industry before Petroleum   46
Chapter 6   Two Murders Intrude upon the Serenity   53
Chapter 7   The Brief Flowering of a South Glastenbury Summer Resort   68
Chapter 8   Decline, Disincorporation and Disappearance   77
Chapter 9   A Parcel Collector and the Viennese Equestrian Influence   91
Chapter 10   Glastenbury, Recreational Mecca, in the News   101
Chapter 11   New Zoning Law Foils Unwise Development   114
Chapter 12   A Twenty-first-century Tour of the Old Ghost Town   117

"Side Hill Farm," by Stephen Sandy   121

Notes 124
Bibliography 126
Index 127

GLASTENBURY

ACKNOWLEDGEMENTS

Several persons have been especially helpful in preparing the text and lending images. Special mention should go to Jim Henderson, Verena Sterba Michels, Mark Haugwout, Rickey Harrington, Tordis Isselhardt, Dick Andrews, State Archivist Gregory Sanford, Victor Rolando, Dr. John R. Howard and others too numerous to mention. Institutions utilized include Special Collections and Bailey-Howe Library at the University of Vermont, the Park-McCullough House of North Bennington, the George A. Russell Collection in Arlington and my own shop, the Bennington Museum's research library. I thank my wife, Ann, for the times this project has tried her patience. Errors, of course, are my own responsibility.

INTRODUCTION

I have been collecting historical tidbits and photographs about Glastenbury ever since I hiked into Fayville in the spring of 1962. The very concept of "hiking into Fayville" promised a certain excitement because I had never before explored a town that was both unorganized and a so-called ghost town. There was, shall we say, a spirited feeling about it. Peering into a Fayville cellar hole, the evidence of a building that once stood more than a century earlier, I took pictures of an array of hinges, latches, horseshoes and other metal objects that surely indicated I had stumbled upon the remains of a blacksmith shop. Returning on several occasions, I have searched for those objects in the same location and never found them. It is probable that someone with a metal detector scooped up every scrap of ferrous metal.

Not long after my cellar hole exploration, I hiked the old Long Trail on an uneventful ascent to the summit of Glastenbury Mountain and surprised a large family of waddling porcupines in an old shelter made of aluminum instead of the wood they like to chew on. They hadn't damaged it—they'd simply taken it over. And standing nearby was Marion Hardy, with her dog. Just to make conversation I asked her, "Is it always so windy up here?" I assumed that Miss Hardy, the retired Bennington County 4-H agent known to be a great hiker, would always be found at the top of Glastenbury Mountain. "I wouldn't know," she replied acidly. "I haven't been here since 1936."

Later, I hiked up the right of way of the old Bennington & Glastenbury Railroad and poked around the former village of South Glastenbury in the cellar holes of the one-time summer resort, the hotel and so-called casino. No trace of the hotel's site can be found today because it was bulldozed soon after my hike as part of a log landing. Remains of the casino's foundation and cellar can still be seen near the flat course of the railroad roadbed. If you know where to look, the ruins of nearly two dozen charcoal kilns can be found, marked by rusting iron bands and, just below the duff, jumbles of bricks.

These two tiny settlements of this geographically huge township, Fayville in the northwest corner and South Glastenbury not far from the Woodford border on the

An aerial winter view from Glastenbury Mountain looks north toward Mount Equinox, *left center*, and Bromley, *straight ahead*. It was taken March 18, 2005, with volunteer pilot Ev Cassagneres of Meriden, Connecticut, flying a LightHawk. *Courtesy of Dick Andrews, Forest Watch.*

south, were never connected by a road. There was no reason to connect them. In the brief time they were both thriving, so to speak, the census of 1880 counted the town's all-time maximum population at 241. Trees always provided the economy, and when the trees were mostly gone, so were the settlements.

One cold February day some years ago I experienced a memorable cross-country ski junket with two companions. We first placed a car near the old airport in Somerset, then came back to Woodford and skied up the former railroad right of way to South Glastenbury. From there we herringboned the steep hill above ruins of the old casino and, after reaching the high point of land and crossing the Long Trail, we cruised down, down, down the vast eastern slopes of Glastenbury into Somerset and back to the waiting car. It had been an unusually cold winter and the streams were frozen and lightly covered with snow so they resembled groomed ski trails.

In 1988 I attended a public hearing in the Bennington County Courthouse when plans for an inappropriately planned community of single-family residences in Glastenbury were squelched by an impressive body of citizens interested in the future of their nearly uninhabited neighboring town.

On another occasion, while I chaired the Shaftsbury Board of Selectmen, I had the opportunity to introduce at least the drivable portions of Glastenbury to Bill Fisk when

A Fayville cellar hole full of horseshoes, hinges and metal objects—obviously the remnants of a blacksmith shop—was photographed by the author in the 1960s.

he was appointed supervisor of unorganized towns and gores for Bennington County by Governor Howard Dean. The office of supervisor changes hands based on the political party of the governor, so when Jim Douglas was elected governor in 2002 the office went to Rickey Harrington, who needed no introduction to Glastenbury because he already lived there. He became the first supervisor in the town's history who was also a resident.

I have served on the Glastenbury Zoning Board, a creation of the Bennington Regional Commission that allows persons who are not residents of the town to be appointed by the supervisor. And I took part in deliberations to consider the addition of one well-planned home and other minor zoning changes. Several interesting evenings were devoted to polishing the wording of an official town plan, under the leadership of the late Charles Yoder and with knowledgeable assistance of Jim Henderson of the Bennington Regional Commission, also the town's administrative assistant.

For several years prior to the 2006 Wilderness Act, Vermonters and other interested parties debated the extent of Green Mountain National Forest land that should be designated by an act of Congress as Wilderness. The proposal was adamantly opposed by snowmobiling and logging interests. I wrote letters to newspapers in favor of a large portion of Glastenbury as permanent Wilderness. My thought was that there are so few other ways in which we in the early twenty-first century can do something that will benefit those living, say, in the twenty-fourth century. This seemed to be one of those ways. Further pursuing that thought: we still venerate those in the eighteenth century who fought for the independence of the American colonies from Great Britain, and we adulate the Founding Fathers who, in 1789, devised a Constitution that has lasted (despite much battering) to this day. As we look back in time, so should we look forward. One problem I have with many politicians is that they are too focused on short-range considerations. It seems to me that Glastenbury is a place where truly long-range planning is appropriate and that a large portion of the land (almost all of it, if I had my way) should be placed in Wilderness status.

During a recent excursion into this venerable town with archaeologist Victor Rolando in early May 2007, I explored the ghost village of South Glastenbury. The skunk cabbage and trout lily were just emerging on a cool, sunny day as we searched for remains of some charcoal kilns that Vic wanted to document for a new edition of his book on industrial archaeology, *Two Hundred Years of Soot and Sweat*. Bolles Brook was flowing too powerfully to allow us to cross it to inspect the kiln ruins, but they could be identified from a distance with binoculars. It was rewarding just to soak in the ambience of the now overgrown site of the brief summer resort that enriched the history of Glastenbury (described in Chapter 7).

It is difficult to describe Glastenbury to those who are not familiar with it and who ask, "What can you possibly write about a town that has a population of six people?" This book is an effort to answer that question.

Chapter 1

IN THE BEGINNING

DUPLICITOUS POLITICS

The fact that the town of Glastenbury in southern Vermont, throughout its more than thirty-six square miles of northern pines and hardwoods, contains a dozen mountain peaks exceeding three thousand feet in elevation starkly conveys its best-known characteristic: uninhabited, wild northern deciduous forest that comprises several vertebrae, so to speak, of the spine of the Green Mountains. Especially in today's overpopulated and overscheduled North American civilization, there is an undeniable fascination with Glastenbury—a place that is definitely low-key and nontechnological. Many find that just the knowledge that Glastenbury exists offers respite and even perhaps a touch of fantasy, even to those who have never actually been there.

Having a single-digit population doesn't mean there is little to be said about Glastenbury. On the contrary, this Vermont municipality has a colorful history of significance, depth and intrigue. As vast woodland with a large official Wilderness component (thanks to an act of Congress in 2006), it plays an important role today in offering outdoor recreational opportunities and providing bountiful supplies of fresh water to surrounding towns.

To start at the beginning and describe the creation, or chartering, of Glastenbury by Governor Benning Wentworth of New Hampshire on August 21, 1761—who was, shall we say, filling a vacuum in jurisdiction—thrusts us into an amazing story. This is the saga of the very founding of the independent Republic of Vermont, which in 1791 became the State of Vermont, first to join the union of the original thirteen American colonies.

One shorthand way of thinking about the Vermont story is to imagine the first two acts of a play, each focused on an important person. First comes Benning Wentworth, who challenged New York by creating many new towns in mostly uninhabited territory that actually belonged to New York. Next comes Ethan Allen who, with his Green Mountain Boys, defended those who purchased land in good faith and settled the towns Wentworth had created. Glastenbury was one of those towns.

The highest of a chain of beaver ponds that feeds Black Brook, which drains south to Fayville. Photo was taken October 18, 2003. *Courtesy of Dick Andrews, Forest Watch.*

The main reason Vermont was the last of the six New England states to be settled was that until the early 1760s this was dangerous land because the French and Indian Wars were still going on. Another reason was that this territory, which really didn't have an acknowledged name other than "the wilderness," belonged to New York, which neglected for a long time to exercise its jurisdiction or to create towns—until Benning Wentworth of New Hampshire did so. The royal province of New York had been established in 1664 by edict of King Charles II, who named it for his brother James, the Duke of York, (hence *New* York) and who drew its eastern boundary at the "west bank of Connecticut River." Look at a map and envision New York State going as far eastward as the Connecticut River and you get a picture of what the early Vermonters were up against.

One might ask what business it was of the royally appointed governor of New Hampshire to start chartering towns west of the Connecticut River. Good question. That's the basic scenario of "the Vermont story." This story, which has amusing as well as geopolitical aspects, focuses on Benning Wentworth, an early American politician about whom the adjectives greedy, manipulative and duplicitous would be no exaggeration. He especially relished jumping into schemes that involved patriotism, religion, expanded jurisdiction, monetary gain and a heavy dash of risk.

Benning Wentworth was born in 1696 to a wealthy family, prominent in New England and old England. His father, John, a merchant in Boston and Portsmouth, then the capital of colonial New Hampshire, was also lieutenant governor of New Hampshire at a time when Massachusetts, Maine and New Hampshire shared the same governor, appointed by the king.

Benning graduated in the class of 1715 at Harvard, where according to his university biographer, Clifton K. Shipton, he set new records for paying fines and breaking windows. Benning then joined the family business, which was involved in a profitable lumber trade with Spain—an arrangement where timber from New England went to Spain in exchange for Spanish wine and British credit. His adversaries would accuse him of selling to Spain the tall trees that were to be reserved as masts for the British navy. That was probably true. He made frequent voyages to Spain and behind his back was called "Don Diego" because he affected the haughty mannerisms of Spanish autocracy.

After his father died in 1730, Benning at age thirty-four soon depleted the sizeable estate he had inherited, and by 1735 influential creditors were hounding him for payment. They came up with a scheme to bail him out financially and to help themselves too. The idea was to have Benning appointed the first royal governor of New Hampshire. In his defense, it must be said that in those days a royally appointed governor often used his office for personal gain.

Benning's predecessor as governor (of both Massachusetts and New Hampshire) was Joseph Belcher, who held him in low regard, calling him "that contemptible simpleton Wentworth," who possessed "pertness" and "insolence and ill manners." Nonetheless, the creditors' scheme worked and Benning was appointed governor of New Hampshire in 1741. He dealt with political adversaries by tossing them plums and created so many local justices that one critic wrote this doggerel:

This was the happy silver age
When magistrates, profoundly sage,
O'erspread the land, and made, it seems,
Justice run down the street in streams.

In 1745, the border between Massachusetts and New Hampshire was adjusted so that several new towns came into Governor Wentworth's jurisdiction, and he sought to arrange for elections in those towns. He had to wait for instructions from the Board of Trade in London, and this led to a political deadlock of several years, so he took advantage of the delay to expand his influence and monetary gain. He chose to presume that the 1731 settlement of the New York–Connecticut boundary, twenty miles east of the Hudson, extended farther north than anyone else had envisioned. He also chose to ignore a confirmatory grant from the king in 1674 following the restoration of the New York province to the English from the Dutch—a grant that gave to New York "all the land[s] from the west side of Connecticut River to the east side of Delaware Bay."

Consequently, in 1749 Benning chartered a town on the twenty-mile line and named it for himself: Bennington. He corresponded with various governors of New York (none

Settlement in Glastenbury was slow and only two of its men were credited with serving in the Revolution. A compilation of Revolutionary participants with Vermont connections, *Soldiers, Sailors, and Patriots of the Revolutionary War, Vermont* by Carleton E. and Sue Fisher, offers only the names of Joshua Elwell, whose service was not identified but was said to be buried in Glastenbury, a town with no cemetery; and Benjamin Glazier, a native of Hardwick, Massachusetts, who served with Captain Billings's company in 1775. Glazier was said to have resided in Glastenbury in 1818, in Sunderland in 1820 and died in 1834.

of them lasted very long) for the next dozen years, first telling them fairly clearly what he was doing. They disputed him, but New York was not aggressive about exerting its jurisdiction in this region. The office of the governor of New York was a kind of political plum in which numerous governors and lieutenant governors had to be brought up to speed on issues, and the matter of this territory between the twenty-mile line and the Connecticut River had low priority.

Benning chartered more towns, violating royal instructions that favored the settlement of more townships, but decreed that they should be no more than six miles squared and not chartered until fifty families were ready to settle.

After Bennington, the next town he created was Halifax on May 11, 1750. He waited a year and chartered Wilmington and Marlboro on the same day, April 29, 1751. Then he gradually locked up the boundary along the Connecticut River and Massachusetts border with Westminster on November 9, 1752; Rockingham on December 28, 1752; and Stamford and Woodford both on March 6, 1753. He kept going, with Townshend and New Fane on June 20, 1753; then three in a day: Brattleboro, Fulham (later called Dummerston) and Putney on December 26, 1753; followed by Chester, Guilford and Tomlinson (later known as Grafton) in 1754. Though "chartered," these towns remained essentially unsettled.

Then followed a long delay while war broke out with France in 1754, a condition that enabled thousands of troops to pass through what was then called the Hampshire Grants so they could sense its attractiveness for settlement. By 1760 and the end of hostilities with the fall of Montreal, Benning lost no time resuming the chartering of towns west of the Connecticut River. But now he let the New York authorities find out by normal channels of communication—for example, slow boats to London and back.

He discovered the advantages of mass production, and in a single day, August 20, 1761, chartered 6 towns: Glastenbury, Shaftsbury, Dorset, Rupert, Springfield and Weathersfield. (The name was spelled "Glossenburry" on the charter, the way it was pronounced in England, and the way some old-time Vermonters still say it.) By the spring of 1764 he had chartered 128 more towns in what today is Vermont. But a governor who signed a sheepskin charter created neither population nor settlement. The charter meant there were "proprietors" or friends of the governor who purchased rights to start selling the land—first links in the chains of title.

When he chartered those towns, Benning had no idea what their topography was like. All he did was draw lines on paper, give names to the resulting squares (mostly of six miles per side) and sign documents he hoped would be taken seriously. They almost weren't.

By issuing plural grants to speculators, Benning had violated royal restrictions on individual grants, to wit: 766 individuals received grants in two townships; 306 individuals received grants in either three or four townships; 151 persons got grants in five or more townships. Samuel Robinson, who in 1761 became the first settler of Bennington, had grants in ten townships. Samuel Avery, who spent his entire life in Connecticut and never settled in Vermont, held grants in twenty townships.

Each town set aside land for religious purposes, the Society for the Propagation of the Gospel, the first minister, a school and of course for Benning Wentworth himself. He artfully named each town for a person of prominence or influence in London. For example, Rupert was named for Prince Rupert who, though deceased, was a national hero beloved by all Englishmen. Shaftsbury was named for the Fourth Earl of Shaftesbury (sic), a member of the Privy Council.

Why Benning chose the name Glastenbury is open to speculation. Perhaps it was for Glastonbury in Somerset, England. The Vermont Glastenbury (note difference in spelling) in Bennington County adjoins the town in Windham County that Benning named Somerset, which he chartered three weeks later. Because he named many towns for prestigious persons with whom he wished to gain favor, it is often assumed that Glastenbury was selected to honor the British Baron Glastonbury. But Esther M. Swift's *Vermont Place-Names* says that this gentleman's name was not associated with peerage until 1797. A possibility is that the town was named for Glastonbury, Connecticut, a Hartford suburb whence Benning hoped to lure settlers. In any case, Vermonters, an independent lot, managed to change one letter in spelling it.

He finally secured the attention of New York officials, who now wanted to establish some new towns of their own in this territory. Some historic maps show a confused overlap of towns created from both sides, New Hampshire and New York. It became clear that what Benning Wentworth had done, in the larger picture, was to create a dispute between two royally appointed governors that could be resolved only by the king, who had more important issues with which to concern himself. Benning, by invoking religion, education and political prominence, had sought to make it difficult for the king to reject his handiwork.

The powers in London first blew the whistle on Governor Wentworth when on July 20, 1764, the Privy Council issued a famously ambiguous decision of the king that declared the west bank of the Connecticut River to be the boundary between New York and New Hampshire. But this decision seemed to mean, to many in the Hampshire Grants, that their titles were to be transferred to New York; and if that had happened, perhaps all would have been smoothed over. But the wording also offered the opportunity for New Yorkers to make settlers pay new fees, an appalling prospect to speculators who owned thousands of acres. In any case, the edict did not reach Governor Wentworth in Portsmouth or officials in Albany for another ten months. By that time, April 1765, there were 128 towns established in the Hampshire Grants, most with settled landowners who were working farmers.

Bennington's pioneer settler Samuel Robinson, also a major land speculator, sought to resolve the stalemate by sailing to London in 1767 to seek the personal attention of the king. But when Robinson contracted smallpox in London and died, resolution was delayed again. Meanwhile, in 1765 the home government in London had caught up with the foibles of Governor Wentworth of New Hampshire and issued a five-point bill of complaint against his: one, neglect of correspondence; two, failure to submit acts for royal approval; three, failure to protect the mast reservations for the royal navy; four, venial land grants; and five, simony (the illicit buying and selling of ecclesiastical favors).

Luck was with him once again. Nephew John Wentworth, in London at the time of this awful development, prevailed upon the king's councilors to allow Benning to resign in dignity rather than face those accusations. Benning got the message and resigned in favor of the nephew, who became the second colonial governor of New Hampshire. Back in Portsmouth, Benning's Assembly, in amusing contrast to earlier disputes with him, issued a praiseworthy resolution upon his retirement after twenty-five years of service—the longest continuous administration in American colonial history!

A couple of personal details about Benning Wentworth, who was predeceased by his wife and all five children (one son, also named Benning, attended Harvard in the class of 1741 and died young): In 1760 the governor, age sixty-four, suddenly announced at a dinner party in his mansion that he and his housekeeper, Martha Hilton, age twenty-four, were to be married. A dinner guest who was an Episcopal priest obliged and married them on the spot. On Benning's death in 1770 he shunned expectant relatives and left his estate to the young widow. She remarried, was widowed again and the fortune was ultimately dispersed.

Soon after Benning's death, amid confusion over land titles and jurisdictions, a new force to be reckoned with arrived on the scene in the form of several brothers from Connecticut, the eldest and loudest being the intrepid Ethan Allen, and the youngest and perhaps most influential being Ira. They took full advantage of the crisis, offered leadership to the cause of the Green Mountain settlers and speculators against the Yorkers. The Allens helped to harass the New Yorkers out of the Grants. Ethan Allen was bombastic, profane, fond of camaraderie and strong drink—a man who rushed heedlessly to serve a cause in which he believed. Shortly after the American Revolution broke out at Lexington and Concord in April 1775, Ethan Allen and a cadre of his Green Mountain Boys captured Fort Ticonderoga and gained the attention of the embryonic nation.

So influential was this act that New York authorities and settlers of the Hampshire Grants buried the hatchet, so to speak, in the interest of unity against the larger enemy, Great Britain. And the official Green Mountain Boys regiment was created, ironically, by New York. But instead of Ethan Allen as commander, the boys elected Seth Warner.

Glastenbury today is one of 5 unorganized towns among Vermont's 251 municipalities, meaning that its population is regarded as too small to justify having a town government. Glastenbury and its sparsely populated neighbor, Somerset, are Vermont's only unorganized towns that ever were organized. (The other three, Lewis, Averill and Ferdinand in the Northeast Kingdom, never had any municipal government.)

The memorable local event of the American Revolution was the Battle of Bennington, which took place on August 16, 1777, just over the New York border and became known as "the turning point of the turning point" of the Patriots' victory. Militia units from Vermont, New Hampshire and Massachusetts, commanded by General John Stark of New Hampshire, defeated the mostly German mercenary forces of British General John Burgoyne. Seth Warner commanded a unit that won a second phase of that battle. Ethan Allen was not there, having been captured by the British in Canada. Burgoyne surrendered two months later after the battles of Saratoga.

Chapter 2

HAPHAZARD RECORDKEEPING

B efore there was any settlement in Glastenbury there were proprietors. These were the land speculators who had purchased rights from Benning Wentworth. They were, for the most part, the same speculators who bought rights in nearby Bennington. Typically, none of them lived in the towns in which they speculated, though there was an exception in the case of the Robinson family, who had migrated north from Hardwick, Massachusetts, settled in Bennington and produced abundant offspring who gained much prominence.

The initial role of the proprietors was to establish "divisions" on the land to determine who had the right to sell what acreage. In the case of Glastenbury, once it was discovered how mountainous the terrain was, the proprietors took their sweet time carving up divisions because it was clear that sales would be extremely slow. The rest of this chapter is written largely because the dry historical records—lost in most towns—are fortuitously available, and the reader will be forgiven for a desire to skip over this material and rejoin the narrative with Chapter 3.

The most venerable of this town's documents are found in a slim, leather-covered volume, the proprietors' "Glastenbury Records and Plan," preserved in a box tied with a ribbon in the Wilbur Collection of Vermontiana at the Bailey-Howe Library, University of Vermont, in Burlington. These records convey a superficial sense of formality, but their accuracy and completeness are casual in the extreme.

Proprietors in most early towns in Vermont kept a rudimentary government before formal organization took place. Governor Wentworth granted Glastenbury to Captain Samuel Robinson Sr. (1706–1767), best known as the founder/settler of Bennington, and to sixty-one other proprietors in sixty-six shares. The proprietors' records suggest that Glastenbury became a kind of plaything with unfulfilled profit potential for a group of lawyers in Bennington some ten miles away. Similar land manipulations also took place in Woodford, evidently with a similar cast of characters, though most of those records have been lost.

As they created "divisions of lots," the proprietors did so by having "an indifferent"—that is, impartial—person conduct a lottery. Such duties were carried out casually and intermittently between 1790 and 1821. In one instance, ten years elapsed between recorded meetings; in another instance, twelve.

The proprietors' records are accompanied by a chart with lot divisions drawn in different sizes and shapes. The original brown ink has faded, and lot numbers are mostly unreadable. The chart was consolidated from earlier records and redrafted in 1883—long after the proprietors had ceased activity—by Edward L. Bates, a prominent Bennington attorney, judge and local history buff, active between 1875 and the 1920s.

Judge Bates's Glastenbury chart is square, which is the correct shape of this town of about 27,300 acres, and it consists of squares and rectangles, with no physical features indicated. Prominent in the southwest corner is the largest, "Govnrs. Right 500 acres," the lot Wentworth reserved for himself, as he did in all towns he chartered. It matches similar rights in the southeast corner of Shaftsbury, northeast corner of Bennington and northwest corner of Woodford, comprising a 2,000-acre contiguous chunk of land for the governor.

Proprietors' records disclose that their first meeting, on June 7, 1790, was moderated by the incumbent governor of Vermont, Moses R. Robinson (1741–1813). One of six sons of pioneer Samuel Robinson, Moses was also the first town clerk of Bennington, from 1762 to 1781, served as a colonel in the militia that evacuated Mount Independence in 1777, belonged to the first Council of Safety that governed Vermont in its earliest days, was the first state supreme court chief justice from 1778 to 1789 and in 1789 was elected governor for a one-year term. He succeeded the first governor, Thomas Chittenden, and in 1790 was succeeded by Chittenden. When Vermont became a state in 1791, Moses Robinson was named one of its first two U.S. senators.

It is not recorded where the first meeting of Glastenbury proprietors was held on June 8, 1790, but later meetings were held in Bennington, often in a lawyer's office. The clerk, the governor's youngest brother, Jonathan, who was also the town surveyor, recorded minutes. His first notation says:

> *Jonathan Robinson, surveyor, under the direction of the Committee for that purpose, of a sixty-acre division for each proprietor, the public rights in sd town.*
>
> *Voted to proceed to make a Draught for the several Lots as mentioned in the plan and for this purpose chose Mr. Gideon Randall and Mr. Asahel Church indifferent persons to make the Draught, which was as follows.*

The "draught" set up sixty-six lots, laid out in two north–south rows along the border with Somerset, listing names of proprietors. Not only are Moses and Jonathan Robinson involved, but also their brothers, Colonel Samuel, Leonard and David, plus another Samuel Robinson. Others are the Lymans—Gideon, Elijah, Phineas, Daniel, John Jr., Roswell and Naomi—who were also speculative proprietors of several Wentworth towns.

Other proprietors included political associates or patrons of the governor of New Hampshire, some listed with their towns of residence. These names, as best one can decipher Jonathan Robinson's handwriting, were:

James, James Jr., Reuben, and Isaac Fray, Richard Wybird Esq., Daniel Warner Esq., Daniel Kittle Esq., Capt. Thomas Martin, Benjamin Stephens, Byfield Lord Esq., Paul March, Silas Pratt, Phineas Pratt, Benjamin Sheldon, Moses Butler, John Fassett, Benjamin Moore, William Moore, Benjamin Whipple, Col. Thomas Doty Esq., Capt. John Nixon, Frederick Home, John Moffett of Boston, Sam'l Gill of Portsmouth, Wm. Smiters of Boston, Bildad Wright, Reuben Wright, Aaron Wright Jr., Elijah Wright, John Wentworth Esq., Benjamin Wentworth, and Capt. John Wentworth of Kittery.

The name Fray is curious. Jonathan Robinson definitely wrote Fray and not Fay. Robinson's sister Sarah was married to Benjamin Fay, a brother of Joseph Fay, secretary of Vermont's first Council of Safety and an associate of Ira Allen. Benjamin Fay was a brother of Dr. Jonas Fay, a founder of the Republic of Vermont. Jonas and his brother Stephen Fay were associated with the famous, or notorious, Catamount Tavern, meeting place of the Green Mountain Boys.

A 1916 letter to the Bennington Banner, signed merely "A Fisherman," knowingly contends that "the once famous lumber village of Fayville" was named for Benjamin Fay, a son of Samuel Fay and grandson of Stephen Fay of Catamount Tavern fame. This letter is worth quoting because it nicely describes Fayville in its prime:

> *It needed but a glance from "Ben" Fay's practical business eye to see that here was a small fortune and that the stream could be harnessed and be made to convert the millions of feet of immense timber into cash, and as a result a mill was built—houses were erected, a storehouse, schoolhouse, stables, etc., followed, one after another, until something like 40 or 50 families made up the village of Fayville which is still remembered by many of the older inhabitants.*

No census of Glastenbury, for any decade from 1790 through 1860, listed a person with the surname Fay. But the first map of Fayville, in the Rice-Harwood wall atlas of 1856, shows the sawmill of "Fay & Cahoone," so it may be assumed that Ben Fay's "practical business eye" remained fixed in history as the little village's name. The 1858 *Walton's Register*, a statewide Vermont yearbook, reports that the only merchant in Glastenbury that year was "Fay & Calhoun, lumber merchants," whose post office was North Shaftsbury.

The first list of proprietary lands included the Society Right, Glebe Right, Minister Right and School Right, all of which, in each town, came to be known as the glebelands. Not mentioned in the proprietors' minutes is the Society for the Propagation of the Gospel, which Wentworth had "established" to convey the suggestion, back in London, that towns he was chartering in the New Hampshire Grants were promoting England's official church.

That first meeting of proprietors voted to raise a tax of nine shillings on each proprietor's right—that is, on sixty-two lots, not counting the four public rights—"for the purpose of defraying the changes allowed for making said division." When the proprietors met again in September 1790, the only action recorded was the election of

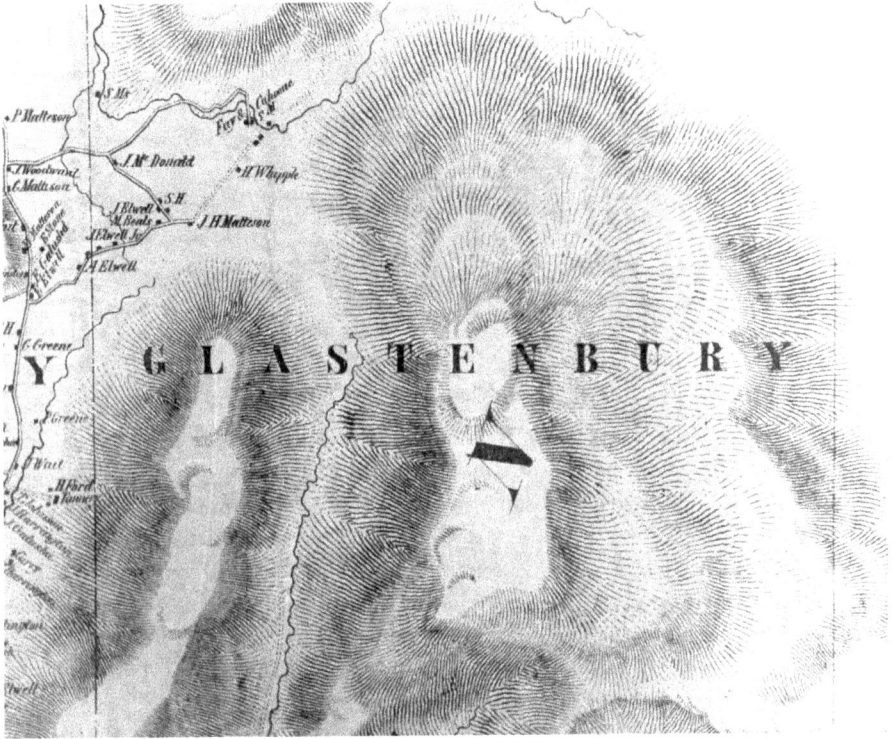

The earliest map of Fayville shows several homes and the sawmill of Fay & Cahoone. It was published in the 1856 Rice-Harwood map of Bennington County.

Anthony Haswell Esq. as treasurer. The prominent Haswell was Vermont's postmaster general and printer, who in June 1783 had begun publishing the weekly *Vermont Gazette*. His name never appears again in the Glastenbury context.

Nearly 5 years went by without another entry. In June 1795, proprietors met to lay out a second division of 105 acres each, "five acres of which to be considered as allowance for a road." Statehood had now been achieved and Moses Robinson, now a United States senator, was again moderator. Others attending were Samuel Robinson, Nathan Robinson and Samuel Whaley. They chose Jonathan Robinson, Samuel Robinson and Peter Matteson (surely the Peter Matteson who built the well-known Peter Matteson Tavern on the East Road in Shaftsbury) as a committee to "make the division." The meeting voted:

> to allow *Peter Matteson the privilege of laying out his second division lot on the original right of Benjamin Whipple on Shaftsbury East line, so as to take in the mills built by said Matteson in Glastenbury as a reward for building said mills, so as not to incommode the other lots, 105 north and south, 160 east and west.*

With that, they adjourned to November 2, 1795. (Members of the inventive Whipple family, who perfected the carpenter's square, were credited with being among founders of the Eagle Square factory in the 1820s.)

The November 2 meeting neglected to approve the second division of lots and adjourned to July 1796; yet no such meeting was recorded. The next entry warned a meeting in April 1798 with an old goal:

> *These are therefore to notify those proprietors and land owners of sd. Town to meet at the dwelling house of Zebulon Ames in Bennington…to accept survey of 2nd Division lots & make a draft for same.*

Meanwhile, Moses Robinson had resigned from the Senate in October, never to hold office again. A meeting on April 2, 1798, at Bennington selected Samuel Hicks as moderator then adjourned to April 12 when Hicks was employed to survey second division lots. Clerk Jonathan Robinson prepared a draft with all proprietors' names, the four "rights" and lot numbers. Then no action was taken for twelve years!

Justice Aaron Hubbel warned a Glastenbury proprietors' meeting for August 6, 1810, "at the house of Messrs. McGowen & Robinson." This meeting, actually held a month later, listed a now familiar cast: Moses Robinson, moderator; Jonathan Robinson, clerk; and Samuel Robinson II, David Robinson, Solomon Safford and Peter Matteson.

Their task was to continue to lay out divisions of lots, to parcel the wilderness town for the first time—a process that had started twenty years earlier in June 1790. Though they neglected to record acceptance of a second division, they voted at this first 1810 meeting to lay out a third division of lots of 135 acres each for each proprietor, 5 of which were to be for highways.

With Moses Robinson as moderator again, a committee of David and Moses Robinson and Peter Matteson was named on September 24, 1810, to lay out a third division and they adjourned to January 1811. But at this point the record deteriorates to a jumble of illegible handwriting and childish scribbling, and no minutes for January 1811 appear.

Instead, the record skips almost a decade to February 14, 1820, and a meeting at the State Arms Tavern, the handsome brick hostelry near the site that was chosen a half century later on which to erect the Bennington Battle Monument. Here, David Robinson was elected moderator to succeed his brother Moses, who had died in 1813, and Jason Blackmer became clerk. Having not met for nine years, proprietors resumed long unfinished business; then adjourned to February 24, when they voted to make the troublesome third division of seventy acres each, including ten for highways.

On June 26, 1820, the proprietors met at "the house of Elias Elwell" and included Solomon Safford, Isaac Webster, Samuel Fay and David Robinson. They unanimously accepted a survey dated June 21, 1820, and executed by Luther Park. (In 1820 Luther Park was an impoverished Woodford resident who in 1823 would father a son, Trenor W., whose name will figure prominently in the Glastenbury story later.) The June 26 meeting voted, finally, "to proceed to the draft," and levied a tax of $152.50 upon each proprietor.

To make the "draft of lots" for the third division, proprietors "chose Job Burt, an indifferent person," to conduct a lottery. Names of proprietors and numbers of lots drawn were listed. The meeting was adjourned again to the State Arms Tavern. Now the minutes, usually taciturn, disclose that in 1821 there are "only nine families residing in Glastenbury," reflecting discouragement that sales of land were so slow. On February 19, 1821, Heman Robinson, clerk pro tem, spelled the name of the town "Glossenbury" as he recorded that it was agreed to lay out a fourth division of lots.

Proprietors met June 25, 1821, to lay out the fourth division, rejected it, then on July 5 accepted it—sixty-five acres each, including five for highways—and once again the names of all proprietors, totaling fifty-six, were listed. They included several Robinsons as usual, a few Lymans, some Frays (still spelled that way, never Fay), John and Benning Wentworth (who must have been descendants of Governor John) and the glebelands.

The proprietors' meetings continued sporadically before matters deteriorated to the point where the legislature, finally, in 1834, made Glastenbury an "organized" town. That act seemed to put an end to the casual activities of the land speculating proprietors.

Finally there is a time gap until it was recorded, awkwardly and undated, in a very different hand, that, "The above named proprietor meeting [*sic*] ever held and thereby

Fayville, from the air in this summer view, appears as an isolated opening in a vast, deciduous forest. *Courtesy of Jim Henderson.*

Despite its high elevation and remoteness, by 1791 the first census of Vermont showed that Glastenbury had attracted thirty-four residents in six families. Heads of those families were George Tibbits, Coffin Wood, Jonathan Clark, Asa Clark, Mathew Fuller and Henry Sly. All were transient, because the 1800 census listed eight different heads of families: William C. Allen, Joseph Blanchard, Oliver Carpenter, Thomas Corey, Daniel Cutler Jr., Joshua Elwell and Ben Glazier (the Revolutionary War veterans) and George Poolex. Only the surname Elwell would survive among future residents. Deming's *Catalogue of Principal Officers of Vermont*, published in Middlebury in 1851, declares Henry and Francis Matteson to be Glastenbury's first settlers. They surely preceded the 1791 census takers. But the name Matteson, usually spelled Mattison in this town, would later be prominently associated with Glastenbury.

Because of its high elevations, steep slopes, rocky and acidic soils, short growing season and formidable climate, the town would always attract settlers slowly. Incorporation in 1834 meant that the town could elect officials and send one member to the Vermont House of Representatives, as did every other town regardless of population.

certify the above foregoing are all the records that know anything about. Attest: David Robinson, proprietors' clerk." To which was added: "I hereby certify that the foregoing records are all that I have ever received. Attest. Luman Hewes, Town Clerk." A last notation, in yet another hand, declares: "Glastenbury April 15, 1890. There has been no alteration or addition to this book. Attest. Jeremiah McDonald, Town Clerk."

Perhaps the best that can be surmised from these enigmatic records is that the proprietors' aspirations for profits from the sale of these wilderness lands were repeatedly frustrated, and as time went on the formalities of proprietorship were given less frequent and more casual attention.

At the first meeting of the organized town in 1834, the following officers were elected: Luman Hewes, town clerk; Asa G. Hewes, first constable; Luman Hewes, Elijah Hewes Jr. and Mark Hotchkiss, selectmen; and Jeremiah McDonald, Harrington Elwell and Mark Hotchkiss, justices; with Hotchkiss as the first town representative to the legislature. As always, in this town, an impressive array of municipal offices was shared by a very small number of persons.

Chapter 3

"A PRETTY SAFE PLACE OF RETREAT FOR BEARS AND OTHER WILD ANIMALS"

This chapter offers a look at what early historians have written, or not written, about Glastenbury over the years, and the story of a prominent early resident.

The first history of Vermont, a remarkably erudite and comprehensive volume, was written by Reverend Samuel Williams of Rutland in 1794 when the state was but three years old. It contains amazing details about natural history such as the mountains, soils, climate, floras and faunas (with much emphasis on the "quadrupeds," or four-legged beasts), but did not mention Glastenbury. The same year he wrote his book, Williams, who earlier had been on the faculty of Harvard College, also founded the *Rutland Herald* newspaper.

Another early history, really more like an enthusiastic travelogue, *Descriptive Sketch of the Present State of Vermont*, was written in 1797 by John A. Graham, an aristocratic lawyer who sought to encourage English migration to Vermont and who offered a town-by-town list of leading residents. Graham lavished praise on the fantastic properties of the soils of various towns and raved about the "prodigious" quantities of crops grown. But he also neglected to mention Glastenbury.

The first description that contained any detail of the town appeared in the appendix to an 1851 volume, *Catalogue of the Principal Officers of Vermont, as Connected with its Political History, From 1778 to 1851*, published in Middlebury by Leonard Deming:

> GLASTENBURY, is near the centre of Bennington county, and the east town in the county, has no post office. Char. Aug. 20, 1761, by N.H. to Capt. Samuel Robinson and 61 others, 68 shares, and 23,040 acres. Org. March 31, 1834. First town clerk, Luman Hewes. First constable, Asa G. Hewes. First selectmen, Luman Hewes, Elijah Hewes, jr., and Mark Hotchkiss. First born, unknown. Jeremiah McDonald has been town clerk 13 yrs. The above are all living. First settlers, Henry and Francis Matteson, a long time ago, but few followed, as the highest population was only 70 in 1810, and 52 in 1850. First justices, Jeremiah McDonald, Harrington Elwell and Mark Hotchkiss 1834. First Rep. Mark Hotchkiss, 1834.

One of the first families to settle in Glastenbury consisted of two physicians, Elijah Hewes and his son Asa G. Hewes, who came from Rhode Island. Dr. Elijah Hewes, who was said to have graduated from the Yale Medical School, wrote a book of medicinal cures titled Female Nurse, and it was published by Asa in Bennington in 1833. Some of his cures seem to rival the maladies for distastefulness.

For jaundice, for example:

Take soot of the chimney, stone soot is best when glossed so as to shine, simmer it in water, and take a sufficient quantity.

Or, to cure whooping cough:

Take mush rat skin, an inch and a half wide, and put it round the neck at night and take it off in the morning if you please. Put it on at night again for four or five nights in succession. This has given great relief.

To cure a rattlesnake bite; that is, when first bitten, according to Dr. Hewes:

Put a bandage round above to prevent the circulation of the poison. Then take a live chicken or fowl and cut a small piece of flesh from under the wing and apply the fresh wound of the fowl to the wound made by the teeth of the snake. As soon as the fowl dies, for it will die very soon of the poison, apply another in the same way, repeat the application of fresh fowls till one shall survive the operation. The poison is then extracted and the wound may be healed in an ordinary way.

For a headache, Dr. Hewes recommended a bizarre combination of drinking pennyroyal tea, binding beet leaves or "horse reddish" on the head, soaking the feet in very hot water, then spreading a plaster of white pine turpentine, tar and ginger onto "the hollows of your feet," plus taking bitter syrup three times a day.

A genealogy of the Hewes-McDonald family says that Elijah Hewes was born in Swanzey, New Hampshire, in 1763, and his wife Lucy Perkins was born in 1776 in Rhode Island. They were among several early settlers from Rhode Island into the northeast corner of Shaftsbury, adjacent to Glastenbury. This family was clearly attracted to remote locations, for the genealogy claims that all three of their children, Elijah Jr., Asa and Martha, were born in Somerset, in 1806, 1808 and 1810 respectively.

This map of the western portion of Glastenbury was attached to Shaftsbury in the F.W. Beers *Atlas of Bennington County, Vermont*. It was published in 1869, three years before the village of South Glastenbury was settled at the terminus of the eight-mile logging railroad from Bennington.

A Glastenbury schoolhouse was among a series of snapshots taken by a Vermont school superintendent, Arthur Wentworth Hewitt, of schools he visited. *Courtesy of the Bennington Museum.*

Shortly after that, Zadock Thompson's 1853 *History of Vermont, Natural, Civil and Statistical* offered a description of each town including an agricultural census, so it provides documentation of the few crops that were grown in Glastenbury:

> *GLASTENBURY, a town in Bennington county, is in lat. 42° 58' and long. 4° 1',
> and is bounded north by Sunderland, east by Somerset, south by Woodford and west
> by Shaftsbury. It lies nine miles northeast from Bennington, and 25 northwest from
> Brattleborough, and was chartered August 20, 1761, containing about 40 square
> miles. A great part of this township is high, broken and incapable of ever being settled.
> Settlements were early commenced here, but the population has never yet amounted to 100
> persons. The waters in the eastern part flow into Deerfield river. From the other parts, they
> pass off to the south and west into the Walloomscoik. The streams are small. Statistics of
> 1840.—Horses, 14; cattle, 16; sheep, 62; swine, 32; wheat, bus[hels], 18; oats, 38;
> rye, 12; buckwheat, 6; Indian corn, 162; sugar, lbs. 575; wool, 127. Population, 53.*

In view of the elevation, long winters and brief growing season it is surprising that even these small quantities of crops were produced.

Abby Maria Hemenway was an energetic Vermonter who became obsessed with the desire to publish a history of every town in the state. She proceeded alphabetically

A couple of old apple trees still grow in the clearing that's now the ghost village of Fayville, where no buildings remain today. The view was taken in December 1989.

through the fourteen counties: Addison, Bennington, Caledonia, Chittenden, Essex, Franklin, Grand Isle, Lamoille, Orange, Orleans, Rutland, Washington, Windham and Windsor. She almost succeeded. When she died without completing Windham it was finished by her sister. Except for the first town, Andover (always alphabetically) she never completed Windsor County. That was ironic because it was the county in which she resided, in the town of Ludlow. The resulting five thick volumes of the *Hemenway Gazetteer*, plus a later index that makes up a sixth, constitute a treasure-trove of histories of nineteenth-century people, places and subject matter for thirteen of the state's fourteen counties.

In Bennington County Miss Hemenway was assisted in her writing endeavors by Governor Hiland Hall, a native of North Bennington who wrote voluminously about Bennington. Hall was the father-in-law of Trenor W. Park, the ambitious lawyer who began a chain of ownership of land in Glastenbury. Hall's description of Glastenbury was written in 1859 and has become kind of a classic, reprinted in several other historical tomes including Hamilton Child's 1883 *Gazetteer of Bennington County* and the F.W. Beers 1869 *Atlas of Bennington County, Vermont*, which offers sophisticated maps of every town and village. After serving two terms as governor, Hall went on to write a serious five-hundred-page history of Vermont from earliest settlement until statehood, published in 1868. Here is what he wrote about our town of interest:

Inside today's cellar hole of the Eagle Square sawmill at Fayville, built during the 1860s, a yellow birch tree stretches its roots to find sustenance.

Glastenbury is one of the roughest and most mountainous towns in the state, and until quite lately has been considered a pretty safe place of retreat for bears and other wild animals. Although much the greater portion of the town is wholly incapable of cultivation, yet it produces abundance of spruce and hemlock timber, which has lately been worked into lumber in considerable quantities, and sent to market. A portion of it goes west, to and through Shaftsbury, and the residue south and westerly, through Woodford.

A small notch of stony land that runs up a short distance among the mountains from the east side of Shaftsbury, has been occupied by a few families for many years. Until the year 1834 they were considered for all practical purposes as belonging to Shaftsbury.

Of Glastenbury, Beers commented, "The town has the smallest population, and the fewest voters of any organized town in the State." Of those voters, Beers said that the town's vote for state officers "has ranged from 9 to 14, always being unanimously given for the Democratic candidates." And this in the nation's then most heavily Republican state, which elected no Democratic governor for more than a century, from 1854 to 1962.

The Beers map shows only the western part of Glastenbury as an adjunct to Shaftsbury, with a vague representation of "Glastenbury Mountain," and just one village, Fayville, in the northwest corner. South Glastenbury, the terminus of the Bennington & Glastenbury Mining & Manufacturing Railroad, near the Woodford border, did not exist when the Beers Atlas was published.

The Beers map will be meaningful to anyone who explores Fayville today, where cellar holes of former buildings can be discerned. Near the junction of the Glastenbury and Fayville roads, the biggest change between then and now, aside from the disappearance of all but one house on the map, has been the construction to near federal interstate standards of Route 7, which skirts just inside the boundary of Glastenbury so that travelers see signs "Shaftsbury-Glastenbury" as they zoom past at more than the legal fifty-five miles per hour in their twenty-first-century vehicles. The state acquired eighty-nine acres in the town to construct this road and right of way.

The only early house still standing is "Chateau Fayville," that of Judge Norman Mattison and his son Ira. In 1869 the house was occupied by "P. McDonald." The Beers atlas shows two schoolhouses, one a quarter mile beyond the McDonald house, the other in Fayville, another mile and a half away. Besides McDonald's residence, the map depicts seven other homes along the western edge of town.

In Fayville, the Beers map also locates a sawmill, powered by flowing water of the Peters Branch, and operations of the Eagle Square Company, headquartered in South Shaftsbury. Remains of the sawmill are evident in a deep stone foundation, and iron bands of a wooden flume can still be seen though the wood itself has rotted.

If Francis and Henry Mattison were the town's first settlers "many years ago," as Leonard Deming wrote in 1851, more Mattisons arrived in the 1840s from Rhode Island. John H. Mattison was an early one, and served as town clerk until 1872. He was also constable, tax collector, selectman, justice of the peace and school superintendent in the Glastenbury tradition. A daughter, Lydia, was town clerk in 1917. A son, John, was a judge and a state senator—the only person ever elected to the Senate from this town.

During the Civil War, when Vermont contributed more men per capita than any other state to the Union effort, tiny Glastenbury, which had a population of forty-seven in the 1860 census, was credited with sending twelve men to the Seventeenth Vermont Regiment. A search for those names, with the help of Tom Ledoux, who operates a website that researches Vermonters in the Civil War, has identified seven of those men to include four Elwells and two McDonalds. They were: George W. Hunt, Clark Elwell, Peter A. Elwell, Newman Elwell, William F. Elwell, Elihu McDonald, Property McDonald and Willoughby T. Vaughan. All survived the war, though Property McDonald died in 1866 and was buried in the Maple Hill Cemetery. The other five men credited to Glastenbury probably were registered in Shaftsbury or another town nearby because Glastenbury, after all, lacked even a post office.

After the Civil War, as Bennington County's population declined and Vermont's as a whole stagnated, the little community of South Glastenbury grew up around a series of brick charcoal kilns and the terminus of the Bennington & Glastenbury Railroad. In 1883 the Child *Gazetteer* listed 30 Glastenbury residents by name but commented, as if to apologize for the small numbers, "Much of the population of this town is transient and therefore not enumerated." But 1880 was also the town's all-time peak, when census enumerators counted 241 residents.

Finally, a meaningful contemporary description of the town is found in the *History of Bennington County* by Lewis Cass Aldrich, published in 1889. The year is significant because it marked the end of the charcoal era, the end of the logging railroad and the start of Glastenbury's decline. After relating information similar to that in the *Hemenway Gazetteer*, and counting the population, Aldrich offered much more detail:

> But with all its disadvantages the town of Glastenbury enjoys benefits such as are afforded to but one or two other towns in this county; it is the northern terminus of what is known as the Bennington and Glastenbury Railroad—not a "trunk line" by any means, but a short road over which is carried every year a vast quantity of lumber, charcoal and other manufactures, the great bulk of which comes from this town. Thus it is that gives to Glastenbury whatever of prominence the town enjoys as one of the civil divisions of the county. The railroad was built during the year 1872. Its length from Bennington to Glastenbury is eight miles. Its construction was considered entirely impracticable by experienced engineers on account of the great elevation to be reached in so short a distance, and the extremely heavy grade to be traveled in certain localities; but, notwithstanding the opposing theories of railroad engineers, the road was built and had been in full operation to the present day. The heaviest grade on the road is 250 feet to the mile on a branch, while the strongest on the main line is some 230 feet. Narrow gauge roads are not infrequently built on as heavy grades as this, but with the standard gauge and traction power this is something remarkable. Better than all, the Bennington and Glastenbury road has been operated with a surprising exemption from accidents.
>
> The manufacturing industry of Glastenbury is confined to the business transacted by the Bennington & Glastenbury Railroad Mining & Manufacturing Company, an incorporated body, the lands of which embrace something like eighteen thousand acres, situated mainly in Glastenbury and Woodford, and some in Somerset Township to the east. In the first named these lands extend north nearly to the Sunderland line. The company has in operation two sawmills, the annual produce of which is about two million feet of lumber, all of which is carried over the company's road to Bennington, and thence to Troy and other large markets in New York State. For the manufacture of charcoal the company operates twelve kilns, situated in the most convenient localities for their work. Altogether about fifty men are employed. The officers of the company are as follows: R.C. Root, president; Amos Aldrich, vice-president and superintendent; Thomas A. Hutchins, bookkeeper and accountant...
>
> The "small notch of stony land that runs up a short distance among the mountains," mentioned in Governor Hall's sketch, embraces whatever there is of Glastenbury's

Tracks of the electric trolley in the 1890s ran beside ruins of four old iron-smelting furnaces at Furnace Grove, near the Bennington-Woodford border. *Courtesy of Images from the Past.*

agricultural district; and this is quite limited. The outlet for that people is by way of Shaftsbury, where their trading and marketing is done. There is no post office in either section of the town, but formerly, in 1873, one was established in the south part and subsequently discontinued. The people of the northern section receive their mail at Shaftsbury, while those in the south part are now obliged to go to South Shaftsbury.

The education welfare of the town is reasonably well guarded, but as for churches, it has none. It is not to be inferred from this statement that the inhabitants of Glastenbury are less religiously inclined than elsewhere in the county, for such cannot be truthfully said concerning them. The population of the town is so scattered or separated, and the circumstances of the people are such that they are not warranted in the erection of a church edifice for any society or denomination, but Shaftsbury on the north and South Shaftsbury below provide accommodations for all who desire to attend at church services.

Aldrich was describing the very beginnings of a permanent economic and population decline, symbolized earlier by the closing of the post office at South Glastenbury. What he did not mention was that the railroad he attempted to portray as such a healthy enterprise was about to declare bankruptcy, and that the trees that produced those millions of board feet of lumber were just about played out.

Chapter 4

OPENING UP "NEW COUNTRY"

THE GLASTENBURY PLANK ROAD

If you can believe a map drawn in 1789 by William Blodgett, there was a road that soared way up over Glastenbury Mountain and down into Somerset. The practical fact is that such a road surely never existed because the elevations involved would have been so severe and so far removed from any other settlements that this speculative detail on the Blodgett map simply makes no sense. If the road, or any part of it, did exist, it has been so thoroughly revegetated that no evidence remains; nor are there any clues in dugouts or cuts and fills that would have to have been part of even the most primitive roadway.

Mapmaker Blodgett was a Revolutionary War veteran from Connecticut, who for two years lived in Bennington where, in 1788, he operated an iron forge on the Walloomsac River at North Street. He drew a historic first map of the Independent Republic of Vermont that offered important details of areas he knew well, like the town of Bennington. But Blodgett left to the imagination other areas with which he was not familiar.

But some sixty years after Blodgett's map, plans were announced for a road not too far from where the early mapmaker drew his line. The Bennington & Glastenbury Railroad Mining & Manufacturing Company had its origins in an act of the Vermont legislature in 1849 that incorporated the so-called Glastenbury Plank Road Company. The ambitious title of this firm was fairly typical of the time, when a corporation wished to cover several possible bases in its name because that was easier than going back to the legislature to redefine its mission. (Today, incorporations are handled through the secretary of state's office.) In 1849 there was potential for mining either ochre deposits or iron ore along the right of way of this railroad, though its purpose ultimately focused on hauling timber. As it turned out, the purpose initially had to do with building a toll road or turnpike, not a railroad. The firm was capitalized with seven thousand dollars by stockholders Lyman Atwater, Trenor W. Park, Silas Wilcox, Samuel H. Brown and Asahel Boothe. The name to remember here is Trenor W. Park.

The Glastenbury Plank Road Company's charter gave it the extraordinary power of eminent domain—so it could take any land required for its turnpike. Stipulations

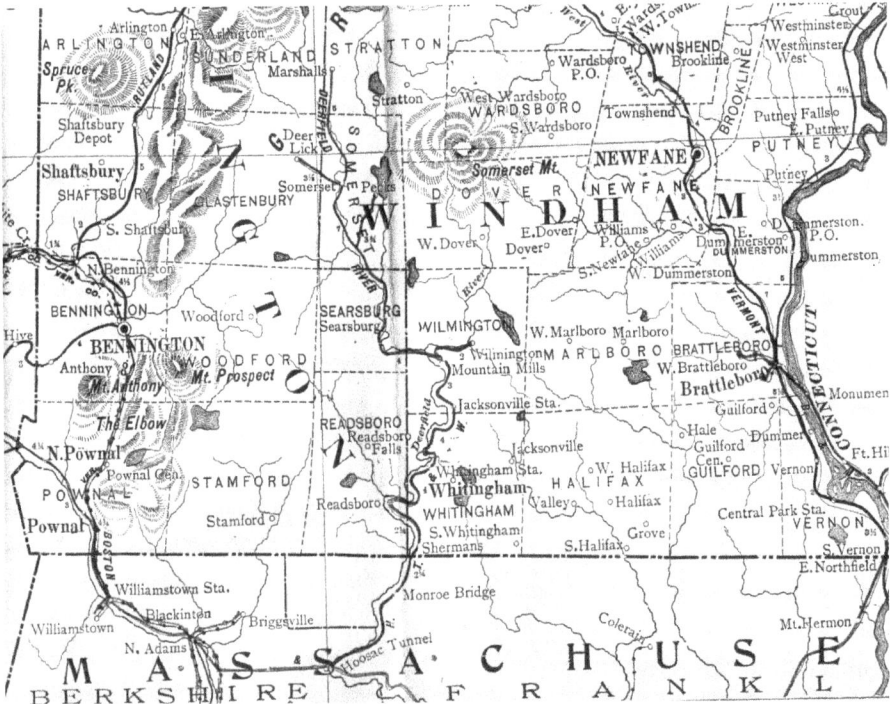

A 1906 railroad map locates Glastenbury in relation to other towns. It also identifies the Deerfield River railroad, a logging line that ran from Hoosac Tunnel, Massachusetts, through the deep Green Mountain forests to a terminus known as "Marshalls" in Stratton, with a spur to "Deer Lick" in eastern Glastenbury. The Bennington & Glastenbury Railroad vanished in 1898 so it does not appear on this map.

included a requirement to post toll rates "painted in legible characters" near the tollbooth, and that its annual profit must not exceed 10 percent of the investment.

In 1849 Trenor W. Park was a twenty-six-year-old Bennington lawyer who had gained that status by "reading the law" rather than by attending a formal course of training. He was married to Laura V. Hall, daughter of the attorney and political figure Hiland Hall. In 1849 Hall was an associate justice of the Vermont Supreme Court and had served for a decade as one of Vermont's five members of the U.S. House of Representatives in Washington, representing the First Congressional District, which then covered Bennington and Windham counties.

In 1852 Park followed his father-in-law to California, where Hall had been appointed the previous year by President Millard Fillmore to the post of federal land commissioner. (Hall and Fillmore served together in Congress and also had family connections in Bennington, where Fillmore's father, Nathaniel, had resided.) Park was seized by ambition to practice law in the gold rush town of San Francisco, and he not only achieved those ambitions but he also profited beyond his wildest dreams dealing in land claims and as part owner and operator of John Charles Fremont's Mariposa gold mine. Over the course of his complex career, Park had interests in several railroads, of which Glastenbury was by far the smallest. At one point he owned the Panama Railroad and sold it at a fortunate time to the French government for a reported personal profit of seven million dollars (in 1880 dollars). After he returned to Bennington from California, Park sought to implement his vision that Bennington could become an important rail crossroads for east–west lines that ran between Boston and Chicago and north–south lines from New York to Montreal. He was outmaneuvered in that scheme and ended up with the so-called corkscrew line from Bennington to Chatham, New York—so named for its circuitous path through Bennington.

The Glastenbury Plank Road Company built a crude road through southern Glastenbury toward Somerset, and the legislature in 1852 let the company extend its road "from its eastern termination through a portion of Somerset, to a point on the Searsburgh Turnpike near Doane's Mills in the town of Searsburgh." This meant that the road the company built through Glastenbury, mostly now long abandoned, still exists in part as today's gravel road between the Somerset Dam and Route 9, Vermont's famed Molly Stark Trail. Doane's Mills was on the Deerfield River at the bottom of Searsburg Mountain near where Route 9 joins the Somerset Road.

The following commentary, written with a curious sense of elation, anticipated the prospect of the plank road and appeared in the *State Banner*, predecessor of the *Bennington Banner*, on Saturday, July 17, 1852:

> *Glastenbury Plank Road:—We are happy to inform our readers that the right feeling is being awakened among those who are interested in the Plank Road, contemplated to be built from this place up through the Northern Valley of Woodford to the south line of Glastenbury and the west line of Somerset,—as already chartered.*
>
> *It is intended, we understand, to continue the road on through the corner of Somerset, to come out in Searsburgh, near Doane's Mills, thus making a new route across the mountain to Searsburgh, Wilmington, Brattleboro, and other places in that direction.*

The article went on to describe the "many favorable circumstances" that "unite to render this burden light." These include the facts that the route itself would cost very little because of eminent domain through wild lands to which few persons held deeds, and that the material for the road itself, the planks, "can be obtained for the whole road for the simple cost of sawing" and did not need to be hauled to the site.

Proprietors of the *Banner*, which called itself "A Family Newspaper, of the largest class," were B.G. and J.I.C. Cook, with an office in the Adams Block, opposite the Franklin House, later site of the Putnam Hotel at Bennington's four corners crossroads. The *Banner*'s editors continued in their praise of the plank road, expecting that it would open up "new country" to development. Of the plank material, they said:

> *The advantages of a plank over common roads are numerous and of a decided character. It is equally good at all season[s], and in the spring and fall, when other roads are nearly impassable, this is as good as at any time.*

They neglected to speculate on what would happen when the wood began to rot or the short amount of time it would take for that to occur.

The road was expected to be completed by "next season." But if it was, any further notice of it in the newspaper has defied an intensive search.

Seriously, can you imagine anything as impractical as a road made of wooden planks, intended to be traveled by horses and horse-drawn carriages? The surface might be all right for a while, but wood of any species laid on top of soil is going to rot. And before it rots, think of the slippery nature of wooden planks in the rain—or snow or ice—on the steep terrain found in the forests of Glastenbury and Somerset.

The road drawn by Blodgett in 1789 should not be confused with the more southerly east–west route known locally as the Heartwellville Stage Road, constructed possibly in the 1750s by the British as part of a Boston-Albany route. The so-called Heartwellville Turnpike left Bennington going southeast along what is now the Burgess road, and continued toward Stamford by way of a road best known for its right angle "elbow" where the route turned east and later crossed the Deerfield River at the southern border of Wilmington.

If the Glastenbury Plank Road was never completed, neither was the next attempt at a transportation line. The Bennington & Glastenbury Railroad Company was chartered in 1855, only a few years after the Bennington-to-Rutland railroad line actually began operations. The intention this time was to build a logging line. The charter identified commissioners of the proposed railroad as Henry G. Root, James L. Stark Jr., Perez Underwood Jr. and Isaac Weeks, all of Bennington, and Jacob Harbour of Woodford. (That last name will figure again in Chapter 6.) The company was allowed to sell hundred-dollar shares of stock totaling thirty thousand dollars, "which may be increased to an amount sufficient to complete said railroad, and furnish all necessary and convenient apparatus for conveyance."

Why this railroad was not built then is a question that must be seen in the context of this new kind of transportation in Vermont in the 1850s. The outlook for extending a line way up into uninhabited mountainous territory was not yet realistic.

But reality had to wait only a decade.

In 1864 the Bennington and Glastenbury Railroad, Mining and Manufacturing Company was incorporated by Russell C. Root, John Harper and Samuel Cornel. Their aim of course was to take advantage of the vast timber resources in Glastenbury. Wood was useful also for the manufacture of charcoal, valued for its even, high heat in smelting the iron ore being mined and processed by Henry Burden and Company in Shaftsbury and in Troy, New York.

An engineer advised that a railroad *could* be built, but the pitch was fearsome: thirteen hundred feet of vertical elevation in just less than nine miles of track from Bennington through Woodford Hollow and up to a clearing known as "the Forks," where east and west branches of Bolles Brook flow together. Improbably, this was the railroad that was really constructed. Legend has it that the first family moved to a new settlement at the terminus of the rail line called South Glastenbury in the frigid winter of 1872. Between

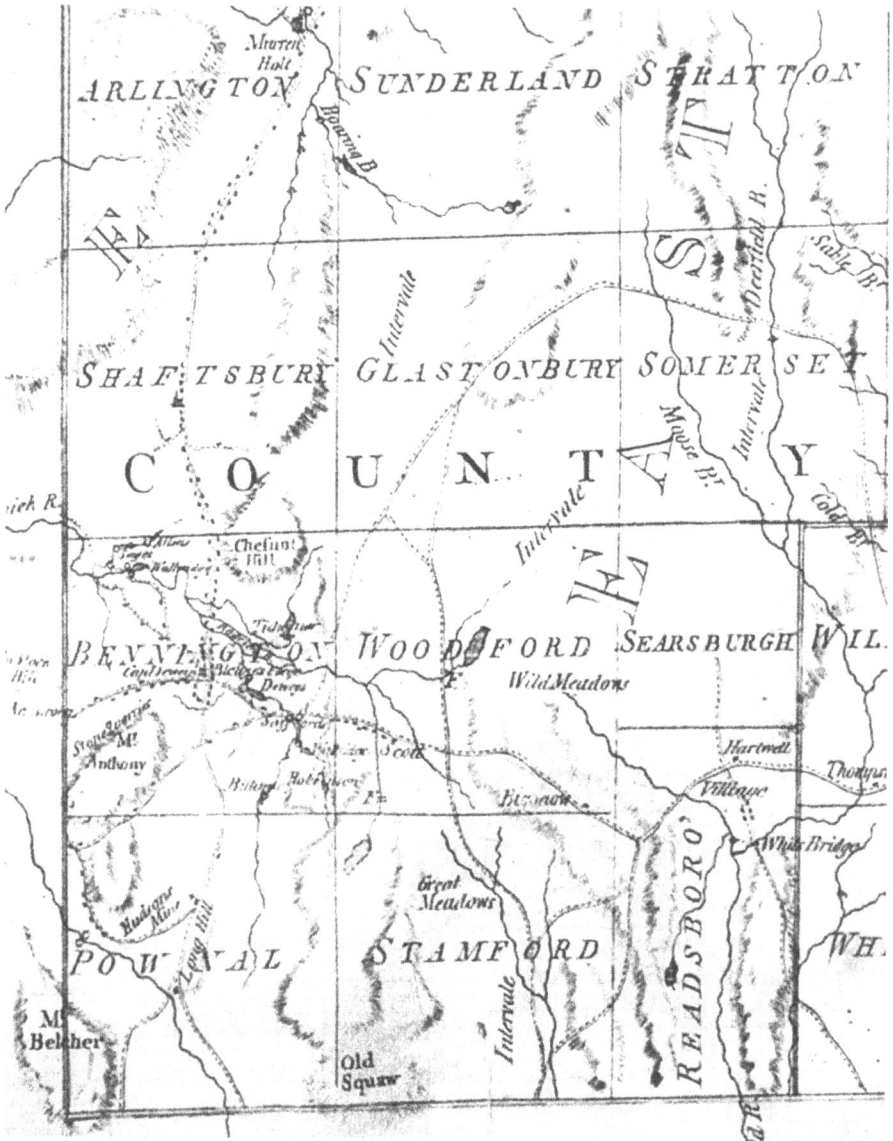

In 1789 mapmaker William Blodgett drew an improbable road going way north in Glastenbury and then into Somerset. Neither town had any settlement in these extremely mountainous regions, and the road seems more speculative than real. *Courtesy of the Massachusetts Historical Society.*

This engraving of Trenor W. Park (1823–1882) was published in the 1889 *History of Bennington County* by Lewis Cass Aldrich.

1873 and 1878 the settlement had a post office, with Charles B. Bradley, an agent of the railroad, as postmaster.

A contemporary newspaper account said that the building of the railroad began on May 1, 1872, and by October the trains were running. The work was done mostly by recent Swedish immigrants, and because the weather was so bad that summer the men averaged only about fifteen days of work a month. The first fatality took place on October 12 when John Vaughn, who was said to have been sleep deprived, fell off the train and it (the train) ran over him. At first, the railroad used wood-burning engines. For a time it used coal, as evidenced by chunks still found along its right of way. The logging railroad line operated until 1889—basically until the trees were all gone, as described in Chapter 3 in the account in Aldrich's *History of Bennington County*.

Later, in 1895 the line was electrified and became known as the Bennington and Woodford Electric Railroad. The electric trolley line was used by passengers who stopped at Camp Comfort, a summer resort on the Roaring Branch in the Hell Hollow section of Woodford, near today's Bennington water treatment plant. It seems counterintuitive, but the trolleys required heavier gauge tracks than the logging railroad. Fewer wheels on the trolleys meant that each wheel carried a heavier load than the cars that carried logs or lumber.

The steep electric line carried a few seasonal sportsmen, hunters, fishermen, picnickers and fern pickers—not really a large clientele. Nonetheless, the picking of ferns for shipment to wholesale florists in New York City and elsewhere did become an occasional profit-making enterprise during summer seasons. Entire families would engage in ferning, loading up their wooden backpacks so heavily they could barely walk. They camped out in abandoned charcoal ovens and lumber shacks.

Indeed, ferning was an activity that lasted well into the twentieth century. The late writer Carlo Wolter of Searsburg and her husband, Charlie Dearcopp, engaged in ferning in Glastenbury when they first retired to Vermont in the late 1940s. Years later she wrote feature stories for the *Banner* and other publications about this summer activity.

The ferns were primarily used for the display of meat products in butcher shops in New York and other cities. Ms. Wolter reported that in recent years the market for real ferns was drying up in favor of plastic ones, which last longer but lack the character of the real thing.

It didn't take too many years for Glastenbury's timber resources to be exhausted. The mountainsides were clear-cut of anything thicker than a sapling. By 1889, when the Bennington & Glastenbury Railroad Mining and Manufacturing Company ceased railroad operations, there were fifty employees. Russell C. Root was president, Amos Aldrich, vice-president and superintendent, and Thomas A. Hutchins, bookkeeper and accountant.

What does one do with an old logging railroad when all the trees have been clear-cut? That was the problem that faced owners of the company after operations ceased in 1889.

A summer aerial view of the forest cover shows clearly why a nineteenth-century settlement was called "the forks" of Bolles Brook. *Courtesy of Jim Henderson.*

Chapter 5

CHARCOAL FUELED INDUSTRY
BEFORE PETROLEUM

There was a time after the Civil War, before oil came into widespread use, when charcoal, laboriously manufactured from abundant trees in remote places like the Vermont town of Glastenbury, fueled a portion of the American industrial economy. Predictably, the phenomenon did not last any longer than the trees that supplied the carbon fiber.

The making of charcoal in Vermont has been researched by archaeologist Victor Rolando, a resident of Bennington, former president of the Vermont Archaeology Society and author of *Two Hundred Years of Soot and Sweat* about Vermont industrial archaeology. Rolando, an inveterate digger into the past, produced mounds of details that form the basis of much of this chapter.

The enormous expansion of the post–Civil War iron industry called for massive quantities of charcoal to fuel the blast furnaces, bloomeries, forges and foundries that produced high-quality iron. Charcoal is a dirty fuel. It is the black, sooty residue of partially burned wood. It required about 180 bushels of charcoal to make a ton of cast iron. Because an acre of forestland yields about 30 cords of wood, which in turn yields about 1,200 bushels of charcoal, that acre theoretically could produce $6\,^2/_3$ tons of iron.

Even before the Civil War, by 1854 charcoal-fueled blast furnaces in Vermont were producing 306,000 tons of cast iron annually, requiring 49,900 acres of forest to be "harvested." By 1870, annual charcoal production was already big business when the Bennington & Glastenbury Railroad began to clear-cut the mountainsides and valleys of Glastenbury, and this gave the town some short-lived economic significance. Indeed, the late nineteenth century witnessed a national scramble for woodlands to convert to charcoal. The Glastenbury-Woodford region became one of three major heavily forested centers of charcoal production in Vermont, the others being Danby–Mount Tabor in Rutland County and Peru-Winhall in northern Bennington County.

Statistics of Glastenbury's charcoal kilns based on contemporary accounts and as reconstructed by archaeologists are impressive. As an accompanying drawing shows,

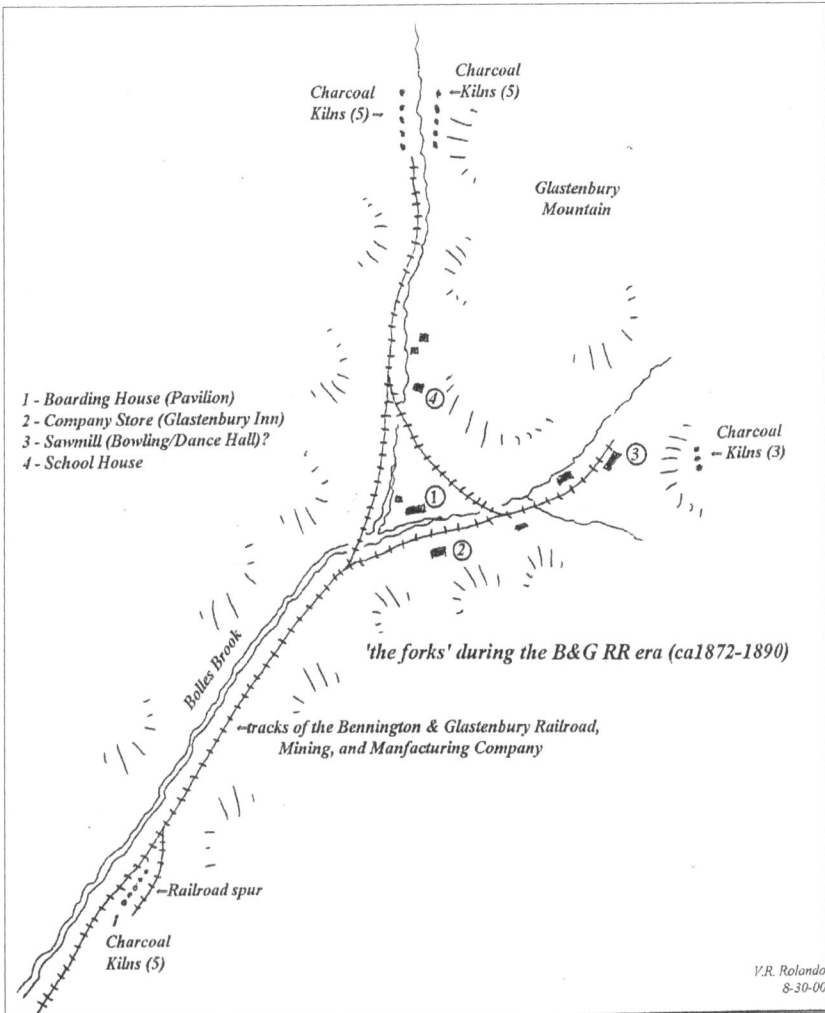

Archaeologist Victor Rolando's sketch marks the location of charcoal kiln ruins near the South Glastenbury settlement at "the forks."

there were at least twenty-one charcoal kilns in or near South Glastenbury, and more are unearthed almost every time a serious search takes place. Each kiln was from twenty-eight to thirty feet in diameter, and twelve to sixteen feet high. It took some thirty-six thousand bricks, double layered and made airtight by mortar, to make a kiln. They were held together by iron reinforcing bands, and had sill plates, top vent liners and doors. Four to five men a day were required to load a charge of forty to fifty cords of wood per kiln. Often, wood not otherwise good for lumber—slash, knots, mill discards—was fed into the kilns.

A haunting view, dating to the 1870s, shows children staring at a photographer next to their primitive log homes. Behind them is one of the charcoal kilns in South Glastenbury with a wood-loading device above it. This is the only known photograph of a working kiln. *Courtesy of Dr. John R. Howard.*

Charcoal was made by allowing the wood to smolder in an environment devoid of air. After a kiln was loaded with as much cordwood as would fit, a softwood fire was started inside. As soon as it took, all doors and vent holes were sealed. Fire consumed the available air, died to a smolder and the wood began to char. Smoldering was controlled by opening and closing small vent holes around the kiln walls. If the wood was allowed to burn, the result would be mere ashes. But charring consumed only the distillates in the wood, boiling out the moisture and resulting in near-pure carbon. Charcoal consists of wood in which all noncarbon elements are removed, therefore it burns hotter than wood, leaving no ash. Being pure carbon, it provides both the fuel to smelt ore and the carbon to make it hard. So it was a valuable commodity.

Charring alone took four or five days, and cooling another five or six days. Thus an entire cycle lasted about twelve days, requiring dozens of workers to tend the kilns around the clock. Records show that B&G kilns yielded about 40 bushels of charcoal per cord of wood—a very good yield—or about 1,600 bushels per charging cycle. The sawmill cut 1,000 board feet an hour and the kilns turned out 28,000 bushels a month, enough to make 155 tons of iron. All this charcoal was hauled out of the woods by rail.

On return runs the train cars carried alcohol to lubricate the workers, some mail, goods for the company store and an occasional passenger. In the early 1880s, the railroad advertised a train leaving Bennington at 7:00 a.m. for the run to Glastenbury, with the return run leaving the terminus at 6:00 p.m. The Rutland Railroad owned

When this photograph was taken, probably in the 1890s, some of Glastenbury's many brick charcoal kilns were still standing. Today they are all in ruins, jumbles of bricks and rusted iron bands. *Courtesy of the Bennington Museum.*

about a dozen special charcoal cars; however, there is no record of their being used by the B&G. Transfer was made at the Bennington yards where bits of charcoal can still be found.

Telltale signs of these kilns today include parts of iron bands that held the structures together, and if you kick the duff you find a jumble of bricks, overgrown by decades of foliage, and an occasional iron hinge or item of hardware.

When the Bennington & Glastenbury Railroad Mining & Manufacturing Company was chartered on November 15, 1864, by Messrs. Root, Harmon, Harwood and Weeks of Bennington, and Jacob Harbour of Woodford, the terms "mining" and "manufacturing" expressed their explicit hopes for remuneration. John Spargo, the founder of the Bennington Museum who wrote about many subjects of local interest, claimed that these railroad officers envisioned all sorts of mining, including the development of great beds of ochre, a mineral used in orange, red and brown pigments.

When the charter was "revived and extended" in 1868, David Love of Bennington replaced the deceased Isaac Weeks, and railroad construction was expected to follow. But because of many problems presented by the proposed terrain—the railroad shared right of way with a brook that ran high each spring—construction of trackage did not begin until after April 4, 1872, when a contract was let to Morrison & Bering. It connected to the Bennington branch of the Rutland Railway line near the corner of today's Depot and County streets, a point near the lowest elevation in Bennington, some

The village of South Glastenbury, ca. 1875, looking south down the railroad line, with a school and workers' housing in the distance. *Courtesy of the Bennington Museum.*

651 feet above sea level. The line ran east through private property along the north side of County Street, crossed Branch Street and began to zigzag across the Roaring Branch. It then passed within a few feet of the long since idle stone furnace stacks at Furnace Grove, and its vibrations no doubt contributed to their deterioration.

At Woodford Hollow the railroad generally ran along the south side of the brook, then turned north along the west side of Harbour Road (sometimes known as Long Trail Road) as it climbed the narrowing Bolles Brook Hollow until it reached its terminus at "the Forks," some 1,911 feet in elevation. So these tracks climbed an unbelievable 1,260 vertical feet in the more than eight miles from Bennington to the Forks. But the tracks rose only 200 feet in the first two miles, meaning that the last three-quarters of the line, from North Branch Street on, presented challenges to the law of gravity that were thought impossible to negotiate at that time.

The first trains ran over a portion of the line in October 1873, and by November the workers had completed hewing the railroad line out of the wilderness. At the Forks, one track continued along the east stream about a quarter mile and another went up the west fork about a half mile. Diagonally across the forks was still another track, about a quarter mile long, that allowed trains to back up from one fork to the other so the engines could stay at the head of the train for the downhill run back to Bennington.

The first Bennington & Glastenbury engine was a 4-4-0, the Housatonic, purchased in 1873 from the Housatonic Railroad in Berkshire County, Massachusetts, on which steam brakes were installed in Bennington. A few years later it was sold to a machinist from Rutland who removed one of the cylinders and sold it to power a sawmill. There was suspicion that the company had another engine that proved too heavy to use, but it was generally accepted that only one engine was used at a time.

The last engine was bought in 1875 or 1876 from the Shepaug, Litchfield & Northern Railroad of Connecticut, the latter's first number 3, named Weantinaug, built by Rogers Locomotive Works in 1871. It was renamed the R.C. Root after the road's president. It remained in service until steam operation was discontinued, and then went to the Bennington & Rutland Railroad as its number 3. After being badly damaged in a collision at South Shaftsbury in 1894, it was scrapped.

None of the B&G engines had air brakes, and the company had no shops of its own. Engines were sent to Rutland—Vermont's railroad city—when they needed repair and a borrowed engine was used as temporary replacement.

Twenty years after the organization of the B&G, after the mountainsides had been stripped of their trees and the tree line had retreated far from any sawmill, the famous blizzard of 1888 shut down the roads for three months. The railroad ended operations in March 1889, and in June the mortgage was called.

Then on November 13, 1890, the Vermont legislature amended the B&G's charter, and eight days later Henry A. Harmon sold the company, along with its rolling stock and fourteen thousand acres of land, to Mason S. Colburn of Manchester, a director of the Bennington & Rutland Railroad, for five thousand dollars. This new B&G Railroad (or "the Harlem Extension," as it was called) saw temporary service over a short section of track at the Bennington end. A few industrial sidings were located near the mainline of the parent company. Remnants of a freight spur still extend easterly to the edge of Depot Street over the former route of the B&G.

When the B&G was transformed into the Bennington & Woodford Electric Railway Company by a charter adopted on November 28, 1894, heavier rails were installed, for weight distribution reasons, to support electric trolleys. Directors of the new corporation were Henry W. Martin, William S. Turck Jr., C.W. Campbell, C.E. Keefe, John Robinson, Amos Aldrich, D.A. Gorton, C.H. Mason and Lock W. Winchester—mostly not familiar names in Bennington. They were empowered to construct the railway by electricity,

> or other power except steam in the towns of Wilmington, Dover, Searsburgh, Somerset, Glastenbury, Woodford, and along the Bennington and Glastenbury Railroad in Bennington to its intersection with North Street, thence along North and River streets to the Bennington & Rutland Railroad passenger depot in the village of Bennington.

In May 1895 work began on replacement of the rails, on reinforcement of old trestles and to fix the roadbed. Electric power came from two steam-powered ninety-horsepower generators in Woodford. Along this trolley line, near the Roaring Branch, were built two recreational facilities by a group of New York businessmen known as the Green Mountain Club (no relation to the later group of the same name that maintains the Long Trail, the 251-mile "path in the wilderness" from Massachusetts to Canada). One was a casino about 1½ miles up from the generating station; the other was Camp

This classic view of the Bennington & Woodford electric trolley has appeared in numerous publications. Motorman Ernest Whitman is at the controls, with a bevy of female passengers dressed to the nines posing for photographer Wills T. White. *Courtesy of Images from the Past.*

Comfort, near today's Bennington water filtration plant. These facilities probably offered the kernel of an idea to others who attempted a more elaborate summer recreation resort in 1897 and 1898.

Property owners along the railroad line in Woodford were not always happy. Families named Shields, VanSantvoord and Godfrey protested the trolley service and claimed that the old steam road was abandoned so that the property should revert to the original landowners. The Vermont Railroad Commission did not support their suit. The attitude of these property owners offered a striking contrast to that of an earlier day. One person who originally provided the B&G with a right of way, for example, is said to have wanted in return for his land not money but only rail passes for his family plus manure from the sawmill horses.

The line's electrician was R.V. Sill of St. Louis, and the first conductors were Ernest Whitman of Arlington and A.E. Raymond of Saratoga Springs, New York. Early motormen were George Woodward of Bennington and Joseph Keenah of Albany, New York. Whitman worked as both a motorman and conductor on the B&W, and later on cars of the Bennington & Woodford Electric Railroad. (Whitman is also a subject of a well-known photograph of the Bennington & Woodford trolley, posing at the controls of an open car occupied by a bevy of well-coifed Victorian women.)

Chapter 6

TWO MURDERS INTRUDE UPON THE SERENITY

The narrative now pauses to relate accounts of two murders and a gruesome fatality during the decade of the so-called Gay Nineties that form an integral aspect of Glastenbury's history and help to lend it a ghostly if not morbid reputation. These dark events also symbolize the start of this town's downhill slide that accompanied the clear-cutting of trees and bankruptcy of the railroad line.

The Crowley murder has appeared in print in various accounts of Glastenbury history, but the killing of John Harbour has never seen public print since details about it were originally published in newspapers in Bennington, Rutland and Troy, New York, more than a century ago.

Neither of these murders saw justice served. In the first, the person convicted ultimately escaped punishment. In the second, there was never even a suspect, let alone a conviction.

To start with the briefest first: the fatal accident. All that is known in terms of documentation is a fragile clipping from a short-lived but energetic weekly newspaper called the *Bennington Reformer*. Dated March 11, 1887, the report lacks even a headline and reads in its entirety as follows:

> *GLASTENBURY—Antoine Sharkey while drawing wood Saturday near the old Burden boarding house, coming down the hill which was icy, he slipped and fell, the oxen running over him with a sled and dray with about three fourths of a cord of wood on it, killing him instantly. He broke his back, ribs, and skull. He leaves a wife and five small children. Two weeks ago Henry Youngs came near losing his life in a like manner near Stockwell's mill. He received several severe injuries as it was.*

Life was rugged indeed in this vast and heavily forested mountain town where the principal business was hauling logs in horse-drawn wagons or sleds. Driving one of those vehicles, uphill or down, you took your life in your hands and hoped for the best.

A slip on the ice or mud, or a free-fall down a steep slope, could mean instant death. Disagreements and feuds among the denizens of all-male logging camps also took their toll.

In Fayville on the evening of April 4, 1892, John Crowley, age thirty-eight, a "jobber" at the Eagle Square sawmill, was murdered by Henry McDowell, aged approximately thirty, another millworker. The instrument of death was either a heavy rock or a chunk of firewood, both plentiful native materials. One version had it that the two were drinking at the home of German Harrington and were returning to the mill when an argument broke out over McDowell's claim that he was a sailor who had run away from the navy. Crowley evidently insisted, "You are not," and McDowell, in his vigor to assert, "I am so," grabbed a stick from the woodpile of Truman Elwell and clobbered Crowley with it.

Another version, according to 1893 *Bennington Banner* accounts, was that McDowell was a deserter from both American and British armies, or navies, who had also used aliases William Conroy, William Lang and William Riley. A newspaper article, calling McDonald "the self-confessed Glastenbury murderer," continued:

> *The region around North Glastenbury* [Fayville] *is wild and thinly settled. It is said that there are not more than twenty-five families in the town. The only employment is wood chopping and charcoal burning. The inhabitants are peaceable and this is the first serious affray that the authorities have ever had to deal with. The town has offered a reward of $200 for McDowell's arrest. Crowley had a brother living in Sandy Hill* [New York] *who was notified of the murder, and he came and took the remains to that village Thursday.*
>
> *McDowell is about five feet eight inches high, compactly built, light brown hair, blue eyes and a sandy mustache. His arms and wrists are tattooed sailor fashion. He is a desperate and determined fellow and will probably make a desperate resistance to arrest. His sailor's uniform is thought to be hidden somewhere around his cabin in the woods and a search will be made for it. His real name and the name of his ship will be found upon the uniform, the authorities think.*

This account claimed that Conroy-McDowell, let's call him, on the night of the murder, had gone to a party in Glastenbury with Crowley, and on returning home became engaged in an argument sparked by some jealousy as to whom was the "real boss" of the town. To quote the *Banner* account:

> *Crowley proposed to do away with all rivals and, producing a large stone concealed on his person, proceeded to attack Conroy. A short, sharp struggle ensued. Crowley was knocked down by a blow on the neck and was so terribly beaten that he died the next morning, never regaining consciousness.*

Of several varying reports, one said he quickly fled the scene, but another, seemingly more reliable, reported that McDowell "took no pains to hide himself" and in fact that he stopped "at a number of woodchoppers' houses" and told them what had happened. To continue with this version in the *Banner*, which acknowledged that its account was "adopted from the *Troy Press*":

> At Cortland Elwell's house in East Shaftsbury, three miles from the scene of the murder, McDowell varied his story somewhat. He told Elwell that Crowley had attacked him with a large stone, and that he had been obliged to kill him in self defense.
>
> McDowell staid at Elwell's Tuesday morning, sleeping on a lounge with his clothes on. There was nothing unusual in his appearance. The only weapon he had was a huge knife, such as is usually carried by sailors. After getting his breakfast at Elwell's, McDowell left the house and went to the home of a woodchopper named Adams half a mile further down the road. He told Adams about the trouble. Adams is employed in the same lumber camp where Crowley and McDowell worked and was just getting his team ready to go to the camp when the murderer came. McDowell asked him to find out how Crowley was. Adams returned to the house about noon. McDowell met him at the gate with the question, "How's John?"
>
> "Dead," was Adams' reply.
>
> "I'm d___d sorry," was all that McDowell said. Without another word he started for the Green Mountains.
>
> Crowley was said to have had $60 in his possession on Monday and his pockets contained only forty-five cents when he was picked up by the Herringtons, yet the authorities are inclined to think that there was another motive for the murder. McDowell's actions ever since coming into the neighborhood has [sic] been very mysterious. He had appeared as if fearful of pursuit and kept to himself as much as possible. Several weeks ago he was heard to say:
>
> "There is only one man in the states who knows who I really am and he will be sorry that he does."
>
> As Crowley knew more about McDowell than anyone else in the neighborhood the remark is thought to have a special significance in connection with the murder.

At any event, McDowell fled the scene, managed to hop a freight train from Bennington to Hoosick Junction, New York, then he proceeded to Lansingburgh, where he was said to have ridden a northbound freight to Jefferson County and on to Canada, where he found work briefly. Finally, he ended up in South Norwalk, Connecticut, where he turned himself in and "made a full confession, his conscience, he says, not being able to bear the burden any longer." But the *Banner* article added ominously, "The prisoner may be playing the insanity dodge. He hears strange voices and imagines that the so-called 'Morrissey Gang' of New York is after him with murderous intent." (The Morrissey Gang was not explained in the newspaper, but his fear may have had some basis in reality. Led by a celebrated New York street brawler named John Morrissey, this gang was one of several Irish mobs in the pay of Tammany Hall in the 1850s that was opposed by anti-Catholic know-nothings. The Morrissey Gang was celebrated in Martin Scorsese's 2002 film *Gangs of New York*.)

Brought back to Vermont by sheriff's deputies, indicted by a Bennington County grand jury, convicted of murder and sentenced to life imprisonment, Conroy-McDowell persuaded the authorities that he was insane and so instead of being sentenced to jail he was ordered to the Vermont State Asylum at Waterbury. He could not have been too crazy, for he was allowed to work around the institution. While filling a railroad car with coal, the canny prisoner hid under a departing load and was never seen again.

Another murder was kind of a Vermont classic—if that's an appropriate way to describe such a family tragedy—because it took place on the opening day of the first statewide deer season Vermont ever held. It was the morning of October 1, 1897.

Although various attempts had been made to protect white-tailed deer in Vermont, dating back to the 1790s, "uninhibited killing in the open seasons," according to a historical study by the Vermont Fish & Wildlife Department, had virtually eliminated the species by 1865. In that year an indefinite closed season on hunting deer was declared. It took several years to replenish the herd. In 1878, ten deer were purchased from the state prison at Dannemora, New York, former Governor Horace Fairbanks donated three more to a Rutland sportsmen's group and four others were obtained "from other sources" and released in Rutland and Bennington counties with the expectation they would reproduce.

Not until 1897 was a statewide season declared for the hunting of deer. The season began on October 1 and lasted for one month. Only bucks could be killed, not does, and no dogs were permitted to chase down the deer. The total official kill that first year was 103, with an estimated 50 more taken illegally. It was the start of a ritual that has continued to this day, with minor variations, though now the deer season lasts for sixteen days beginning on the second Saturday of November.

On the opening day of that first deer season in 1897 a prominent citizen of Woodford, John Harbour, age forty, married and the father of four children—Lura, Guy, Polly and Amy—was shot and killed while hunting in Bickford Hollow, a remote section of Glastenbury. No one was ever accused as the killer, let alone tried or convicted. Was John Harbour mistaken for a deer? Was he the victim of some kind of grudge killing? The victim was said to be well liked, and no evidence for deliberate murder was brought to light. The case was simply never resolved, but then it didn't seem to have been investigated very thoroughly either.

Because the victim's grandson, Dr. John R. Howard of Edelstein, Illinois, has provided this writer with extensive irreplaceable clippings from the *Bennington Reformer*, and because the story was so dramatically reported, we are going to let that newspaper tell most of the story of the death of John Harbour. These clippings are virtually unique because no copies of the *Bennington Reformer* for this era are known to exist in any library or on microfilm. Though lengthy, the unbylined article is well written, contains amazing detail and it conveys not only the nature of the remote upland flanks of Glastenbury, but it also describes the preparations taken by serious hunters at the time of Vermont's first ever statewide deer season—and it conveys the shock of the community that such a tragic event could occur with no resolution.

Above: The "Frenchman's shanty," where John Harbour camped while deer hunting in Glastenbury's Bickford Hollow region. Shown is John's brother, Harry Harbour. *Courtesy of Dr. John R. Howard.*

Right: A tintype of John Harbour, who was killed on the opening of Vermont's very first statewide deer season, October 1, 1897. *Courtesy of Dr. John R. Howard.*

The extensive *Reformer* coverage of this case was unquestionably written by its editor/ publisher James H. Livingston, a peripatetic and sometimes apoplectic newspaperman. Livingston had worked on, or partially owned, weekly papers in Cambridge and Hoosick Falls, New York; Rutland, Vermont; Lynn and Greenfield, Massachusetts; and in 1882 he took a half interest in both the *Brattleboro Reformer* and *Bennington Reformer*. He dissolved a partnership in 1883 and took over the *Bennington Reformer*, which became an antagonistic competitor to the *Bennington Banner*. In 1902 both papers merged after acquisition by Frank E. "Ginger" Howe, who dropped the name *Reformer* and upgraded the *Banner* in 1903 from a semiweekly to a daily—which it remains today.

The small one-column headline of Livingston's *Bennington Reformer* on Friday, October 1, 1897, said, "First Victim of the Chase," with a subhead that read: "John Harbour Shot and Killed on the Green Mountain—Probably Taken for a Deer—The Man Who Fired the Shot Unknown—Body Found After Long Search." And the story, which appears here with its original spelling and style, reads as follows:

> *Wilton A. Viall, the Main-St. merchant, John and Harry Harbour, brothers, of Woodford, started out yesterday afternoon for the Green Mountain range in order to be on the ground at the opening of the deer season. They went up Woodford Hollow till they struck the Bickford Hollow, which they followed for a short distance, struck a wood road and climbed to the summit of the mountain on the east. Following the crest of this spur, they finally came to a woodman's shanty at a point opposite and north-west of the Glastenbury club-house, and on the west of the left hand branch. Here they located. While Harry Harbour remained at the shanty to prepare supper, John Harbour and W.A. Viall started out to see if they could locate deer runs. It was nearly dusk at the time. They took divergent directions, and had gone but a short distance from the shanty when Viall heard the report of a gun. A moment later he heard somebody shout "I've shot him!" or "I'm shot." Viall called but got no answer. Then he hurried back to the shanty and got the brother Harry and a lantern and they searched the woods together, shouting from time to time. There was a dread suspicion all the time that a tragedy had been committed. Finally it was arranged that Harry Harbour should take the lantern and return to the Hollow for help. This he did, getting down into civilization at about 11 o'clock at night.*
>
> *After ten or a dozen men had been roused up from their beds the party returned to the shanty and hunted all night with lanterns for the missing man.*
>
> *At 4 o'clock this morning Geo Shurtleff and N.F. Smith, with guns and ammunition, started from the village here for the same location also to hunt deer. They reached the scene in time to join in the hunt for the missing man.*
>
> *At about 11 a.m. the body was found under a spruce tree whose limbs nearly dragged on the ground. Only the feet were visible. The spot was not far from where the shot was heard the night before. The dead man lay stretched on his back on the ground, with his loaded gun beside him. Did he crawl there after being shot? Hardly. Neither could he have fallen dead upon the spot. There's the mystery. Did another party—and the evidence that another party had camped near by—take him for a deer, but finding their mistake, seek to hide the body? Who can say?*

The bullet had entered the body about two inches above and to the right of the right nipple, and passed straight through and out at the back of the body. An autopsy will disclose whether death was instantaneous. Undertaker Walbridge was notified by Shurtleff and Smith, who came directly back to the village, and the necessary burial outfit was immediately set up.

The body was brought down off the mountain on an improvised stretcher to his house near Camp Comfort. Drs. Rogers, Goodall [unreadable] have gone to the home [unreadable] autopsy.

John Harbour was about 40 years old and leaves a family. He was a son of Jacob Harbour. He leaves five brothers and three sisters. They are Harry, Giles, Grant, Charles, and Mark, Mrs. Geo. F. Townsend and Rose Harbour of Bennington, and Mrs. John Hathaway of Pownal.

That was the initial report in the *Bennington Reformer*. The competing paper, the *Bennington Banner*, covered the tragedy in much more brief format, and with some different facts. Whereas the *Reformer* said the victim had been struck through the upper chest and was stretched out beneath a spruce bough, the *Banner*'s account had him killed by a bullet to the head and said the perpetrator propped him upright in a sitting position with his back against a tree. They agreed that the victim's loaded gun was left by his side.

A full week later, on Friday, October 8, the mostly lengthy article appeared in the *Reformer*, divided into five chapters, following this brief funeral notice:

The funeral of our esteemed and beloved townsman, John Harbour, was attended from his house Monday afternoon by a large concourse of people. The Rev. Atwell officiated in an able manner from the text, "But now we see through a glass darkly." There are many who mourn besides the near and dear relatives of the departed.

Then followed the long article, headlined "The Murder of John Harbour," with a descriptive subheading, "He Who Sped the Fatal Bullet Confesses the Crime of Murder by His Silence—Guilt Hides Behind the Mask of Subterfuge, while Innocence Has Nothing to Conceal—It was Murder, Not Accident, Hence the Mystery." An introduction preceded the five "chapters," as follows:

No living man, born of woman, and being endowed with common intelligence, could innocently or accidentally take human life and seek to conceal the act from his fellowman. There are various degrees attached by statute law to the taking of human life. Murder is to take life with malice aforethought or prepense, express or implied; manslaughter is murder without malice, express or implied, and this may be voluntary, upon a sudden heat or excitement of anger, or involuntary, but in the commission of some unlawful act. Then there is justifiable homicide, when life is taken in self-defense, and killing under various circumstances recognized as legitimate by the law. But when life is taken innocently and the deed concealed, then the act of concealment is taken and weighed as prime facie evidence of willful murder.

GLASTENBURY

Chapter I.

W. A. Viall, a leading merchant of Bennington, had laid plans with John and Harry Harbour, brothers, of Woodford, to go into the Glastenbury mountains to hunt deer. The trio had previously gone into the mountains and selected their stamping grounds.

The location was on the ridge of the range running north and south that forms the west side of the valley through which trends the Woodford electric [railroad], *and about as far north, but nearly two miles west, of the Glastenbury club house. The ridge of this range is very uneven, and all in all it is as rugged and primeval in rank vegetation as a tropical jungle, minus the hanging vines. There is level ground there, fully a mile and a half in length, and an old orchard whose fruit is garnered annually by bruin alone, the last mournful evidence of a once thrifty farm now returned to nature whence it was wrested more than a century ago. And there are lowlands and highlands—swamps and eminences. There is a little cleared land—swept clean by forest fires—some brush land and much wooded land. An old Frenchman is domiciled in a shanty there and chops cordwood for Harry Harbour, who owns the stumpage.*

Thursday afternoon last Viall packed his provisions, arms and ammunition in a [unreadable] *wagon and was about to unhitch his horse from the post in front of his store and start for the mountains when he was called by W.H. Bradford to go over to the latter's barn. Viall had broken his own gun and borrowed of Howard Shields an old style, double-barrel, English pin-fire gun. Bradford insisted on Viall taking the former's Winchester, a 44-caliber, 16-shot rifle, and a box of 50 cartridges to fit it. Viall took both guns on to the mountain.*

Arrived at John Harbour's house, just above Camp Comfort, Viall found that John was not ready to start then and Harry had not returned from the village. Viall drove on alone. A few roads beyond Harbour's on the left, opens a broad ravine down which a brook tumbles fretfully. This is called Bickford hollow. Opening a gate and following a private road a short distance, a bridge is crossed on the right, and then by a very fair wood road the ascent of the mountain is begun. When well up on the mountain Viall halted his horse for a breathing spell. He was soon overtaken by Will Robinson, a farmer of the west part of the town, and his hired man, Frank Smith, a native of Woodford, who is accounted one of the best woodsmen in all this region and who knows practically every foot of all those mountain fastnesses, one who, indeed, has chopped wood on this very range more than one season and hunted it over and over again. Viall spoke to the men as they approached him. They had their guns in their hands and their camp equipage strapped on their backs. Before Robinson and Smith quite reached him, Viall drove on, and after a time found himself on a wrong road, which he had to retrace some distance to connect with the right one. In the meantime Robinson and Smith had passed him or turned from the direct road to the Frenchman's cabin. Viall did not see them again thereafter.

Arriving at the shanty, Viall unharnessed his horse and hitched it to a tree near by, then unloaded his truck and stored it in the building, standing his double-barrel gun in one corner. It was then about 4 o'clock. Being alone and having about two hours to spare before dark, he took the Winchester rifle, loaded in three shells and started for the "burnt place," a knoll nearly a mile east of the shanty and the spot assigned him to occupy in the still hunt. It was ahead of the law as to time by about eight hours, but quite excusable under the circumstances. Reaching the spot he was to occupy, Viall waited for a noble buck to come along and get plugged. It didn't come—to any appreciable extent. Presently Viall heard the sound of chopping, as of someone felling saplings, trimming them up, sharpening them into stakes and driving them into the ground. The sound came from the north-east, a quarter of a mile or more down toward the Glastenbury club house, near a swamp where there is a good spring of water. Viall made no doubt that Robinson and Smith were down there arranging their camp. And still he waited and longed for the coming of the buck that yet tarried out of sight. Then, looking across to the north, Viall saw John Harbour with his gun laboring up a wood road that led to his allotted station on a knoll about a quarter of a mile away. Harry and John had come up to the shanty together, arriving at about 5 o'clock. John saw the Shields gun that Viall had left standing in the corner of the shanty, picked it up to examine it, and said he would take it out and try it if he got the chance. John and Harry started out together, but the latter soon concluded to return to the shanty and prepare supper.

As it was growing dusky now, and Viall, not any too well acquainted with the territory, started for the shanty, hoping to make it before utter darkness fell upon the path. He had traversed possibly a quarter of the distance when a rifle shot rang out on the startled air and reverberated through the mountain peaks; and still it was not the sharp crack of the ordinary rifle, nor yet the heavier boom of the shot gun; it was very like the sound evolved from the discharge of a Winchester. Viall stopped on the instant, and then came across the valley the horrified, and horrifying cry, "My God, you have shot me!" or, "My God, I am shot."

It was John's voice. Had he shot himself or been shot by another? He was in trouble in either event. Why did Viall not go to him at once and lend him aid? you will ask, as hundreds of others have querried. It was now almost dark, even in the clearing. It was utterly dark in the intervening woods, and Viall was a stranger to them. He would hurry to the shanty, summon aid, or at least secure a lantern. He stumbled over the rough ground at the top of his bent, while it grew momentarily darker. When he thought he had lost his way in his great excitement, because his anxiety had outrun his footsteps, he heard the sound of pounding and knew it came from within the shanty. It was Harry driving nails to hang their coats on. Then Harry heard the horses floundering around outside and stepped to the door as Viall, out of breath, reached the shanty. Had John returned? No? Then he must be in trouble. The facts were detailed hurriedly, the lantern lighted, and the two set out in quest of John, leaving the old Frenchman to finish getting supper.

The spot where Viall was brought to a halt by the shot that sped the fatal bullet was first visited in order to locate the point from whence the sound came. Then they went straight across the intervening depression to the rise of ground beyond. There they hunted for more than an hour, shouting at the tops of their voices, "John! John!" without reply, save from the echoes that wailed back to them through the tree tops as if in mockery, "John!" John, if hurt, had struggled back to the shanty by this time. They would take the route that John had probably taken, and search carefully all the way back. But John was not returned. The supper stood ready to be spread smoking hot on the rough table, and the searchers were wearied and famished almost to utter exhaustion, but John was still out in the silent and somber wood, wounded and helpless, perchance watching through the spectral tree tops the cold stars in God's great firmament while his life blood ebbed away. They would find and succor him.

Another hour was spent in fruitless search. A broad area was gone carefully over, every bush uplifted that might conceal a human form, and every shadow that promised evidence under the lantern's fitful glare was investigated. All to no avail. Harry would saddle his horse and go down into the valley below for help. It was four miles away, over a hard and uneven wood, and it was near 11 o'clock when he reached civilization.

Chapter II.

It was just possible that John, wounded, had found it advisable to come off the mountain and get where medical aid could be more readily summoned. He had not reached his house, was the startled words [sic] *of an agonized wife. Then the alarm was sounded from house to house down through the valley, and a party of eight or ten mountaineers was soon wending its way up the precipitous mountainside, the lanterns glimmering through the forest trees like will-o'-the-wisps at hide and seek. It was an anxious little band. Every one of them knew John—had known him since boyhood, for he was born there and had lived all his forty years of life among them. His grandfather had owned and farmed the very land on which he had gone to hunt that day. John Harbour was a man of strict honesty and integrity, and his neighbors loved and honored him accordingly.*

It was 3 o'clock in the morning when the exhausted little band of searchers turned in at the shanty and lay down to snatch some rest and sleep before the break of another day. They had seemingly searched every foot of each all around the place where apparently John must be, unless he had wandered aimlessly away, or fallen down somewhere in his efforts to leave the mountain and gain his home.

It was daylight when the search was renewed. It was 11:30 o'clock when the body was found, cold in death. There were 36 men in the searching party then. They had formed a skirmish line, fifteen feet as near as might be between man and man, and three several times they had swept up and down along the ridge of the mountain, covering more than a mile square of area without result. It was thought that every inch of ground, hidden or exposed, had been scrutinized. The searchers were nonplussed and discouraged. They were at a standstill. Then it was suggested by somebody that a skirmish line be formed at right angles with the first lines and every hidden spot be approached by flank movement. The very first time the line swept over the crest of the mountain the body was found. But a single foot was exposed. Young Fred Smith, called by his associates "the ferret," because he always fills his kreel when he fishes and his bag when he hunts, and seems to know the choicest game abides, was the discoverer. Well up in under the boughs of a spruce tree, one of a clump, whose limbs fairly swept the ground, lay the mortal remains of poor John. The body was as though laid out by careful hands before rigor mortis had set in. Prone and at full length on the back, arms straight and close to the body on either side, hat on head and gun with the muzzle uppermost laid carefully along side. There is a serene look on the countenance, indicating that death had not tarried long nor inflicted much physical or mental pain. A stretcher of saplings, over which blankets are folded, is improvised, the body laid tenderly thereon and moving hands bear the remains down the winding mountain road and over the threshold of a devoted home where there is grief and agony and broken hearts and scalding tears, and peace and comfort only for the dead.

Chapter III.

Frank Smith, native of the Green Mountains, and his employer, Wm. Robinson, was a member of the late firm of Bassett & Robinson, but now runs his father's farm out west of the Center [Old Bennington] *village, was driven with their traps by Jesse Robinson, the father, and set down at the mouth of Bickford hollow last Thursday afternoon. They had blankets to sleep under, a hatchet and a lantern, a store of cold chicken and wholesome farm provender enough to last them till Saturday night or Sunday morning. They strapped their packs on their backs and started up the mountain road.*

Jesse Robinson returned to the village. On his way home he stopped at Bassett's grocer. Mr. Bassett is his son-in-law. He told that the boys were going in a mile or more beyond the Frenchman's shanty; they took blankets along because they would have to sleep out of doors; they knew that Viall and the Harbour brothers would occupy the shanty; they had their ground all laid out; Smith had been up there more than once to locate the likeliest habitat of the deer; they would bag some game sure.

At a little after 7 o'clock that night an electric car was pushing a dumpy load of coal up the road to the Glastenbury inn. When near the "five kilns," and directly opposite the Lute Evans bridge, where the boys held a clam bake last year, a fuse blew out. The trainmen were fixing it when the fitful flickering of a lantern was seen on the wood road across the bridge. The trainmen shouted to the bearer of the light and instantly it went out. There was no reply. This wood road leads directly up to the vicinity of the "burnt piece," where Viall stood.

At 4 o'clock Friday morning Dr. Shaw and a man named Stemp of Hoosick Falls, accompanied by Jim Higgins and a German named Shoults of Woodford City, started from the City for Castle Meadows. They reached their destination between 8 and 9 o'clock, just as Robinson and Smith also arrived there. They met and talked together a few moments. Then they parted. Dr. Shaw noted and remarked later that Smith appeared highly excited about something; like one who is in flight from justice. He seemed anxious to get away from them; he would look no man in the eye.

At 3 o'clock Saturday afternoon Robinson and Smith came out over the old tramway from Pine valley, trudged down through the City to the Hollow and took an electric car for Bennington. They learned on the way that they were wanted by the authorities. They gave themselves up to Deputy Godfrey, who took them before Judge Darling. Smith particularly was highly excited and could not give a very satisfactory explanation of his wanderings on the mountains. The judge told them to go home and return again on Monday. The judge expected that the truth would come out then. But on Monday they had settled down to one story; it had some "blow holes" in it, however. For instance, it took nearly two hours longer to get down off the mountain by the shorter route than it took to get up it by the longer route; they intended to hunt on ground north of the shanty, but seeing the smoke from the camp fire near the spring at the edge of the swamp, they concluded to keep right on, and came out near the club house, went up the right hand fork to the Harris mill, some four or five miles away, where they passed the remainder of the night, and went into Castle meadows in the morning.

Chapter IV.

Friday afternoon Judge Darling and State's Attorney Bates drove up to the scene of the tragedy. There were many others there. The ground was carefully gone over. The spot where Harbour fell when he was shot was located. There was some blood on the ground, and the clotted turf was taken up and brought away. From this point the body had been dragged about 70 feet directly toward the swamp, then hidden carefully away. The camp by the spring near the swamp was located. Two sapling crotches had been cut and driven into the ground, a cross-stick laid on and by a mark on this stick it was evident a tin pail had been hung to cook coffee. On the ground underneath were the ashes of a very small fire. Some chicken bones lay about. Near by was a bunch of golden rod which had evidently been gathered for bedding. Down the Lute Evans wood road, near the electric track, foot prints were found. They were of two kinds, one round toed and the other long toed. The men who occupied the camp, but abandoned it in haste in the early evening, came off the mountain by this road. Robinson and Smith claim that they left the mountain by a road farther to the north. One of the men who built that camp by the spring near the swamp killed John Harbour. Probably the killing was accidental. The keeping of the secret along points to deliberate murder. It probably happened in this way: Like the other party, one or both the men of the little camp went out to watch for a shot; it finally grew dusky; John wore a snuff colored hunting jacket; he had started for the shanty; in the uncertain light he was taken for a deer and shot; the bullet was doubtless from a Winchester, because it entered the breast just above and to the right of the right nipple and passed clear through the body, shattering the ribs both front and back; a Winchester throws a ball like that; the cry of pain revealed the horrible mistake; they man went to the fallen hunter; picked him up with an intent to succor him; dragged him toward the camp for a distance; found presently and to his horror that he was dead; then he lost his wits; hastily concealing the body he rushed back, broke camp and hurried with his companion off the mountain.

Who shot John Harbour? Viall had a Winchester rifle, 44 caliber; Smith had a Winchester rifle, 45 caliber. Either gun would have done the business. Was there another Winchester on the mountain that day? Happily Viall had realized that suspicion might rest with him, so he had given Harry Harbour his gun to examine. It had not been fired since it was cleaned. There were three shells in the magazine. These were pumped out and put in the box, then all were counted twice over. There were 50 of them. Viall was innocent.

Who shot John Harbour? The Reformer would not willfully accuse anybody. It looks fearfully like Smith, but Smith says "No," and Robinson says "No." And still they had

Two Murders Intrude upon the Serenity

gone that day to hunt deer on ground laid out a long time in advance; on ground known by Smith to be the likeliest on the mountain. They had ridden six miles and walked four more hard miles to reach this ground, and just because they saw smoke from a little camp fire not so big as their hat, they concluded, late as it was in the day, to cross over to the east mountain, seven miles away—seven miles of fearful tramping, especially with a lantern in the night.

Who killed John Harbour?

Chapter V.

The funeral services over the remains of the late John Harbour were held from the little home in the Hollow at 3 o'clock Monday afternoon. A large number of friends of the deceased was present. Rev. J.L. Atwell preached the sermon from the text, "But now we see through a glass darkly." The remains were taken, by his five surviving brothers, Charles, Harry, Mark, Giles, and Grant, to the grave in the little family burying ground on the terrace overlooking the old homestead and the valley in which John had passed all his 40 years of life, and laid them away.

Robinson and Smith attended the funeral services and looked tranquilly upon the face of the dead.

Who KILLED John Harbour?

Whether other news articles appeared in the interim is not certain because archival copies are not available, but the next known report is dated Friday, November 26, some seven weeks after the lengthy five-chapter summary. Livingston, the assumed author, rose to heights of verbal self-flagellation. Again, this one-paragraph article appears here with its original spelling and style:

Friday, November 26, 1897:

Who killed John Harbour? It seems a late hour in the day to make the inquiry, but we note that the state's attorney has been summoning witnesses and holding further inquest with a view to clearing up the mystery surrounding this tragedy. It is understood that no tangible evidence upon which to hang a charge against anybody has been secured, and therefore the guilty are to go unwhipt of justice. We may be wrong about it, but we think that the proper time to have acted was at the time of the shooting. We should have got possession of the patch of cloth that was torn from the clothing of the man who assisted in dragging away and concealing the body of the dead hunter—the patch of cloth that was found on a jagged oak near by. We should have found the shoes that fitted the tracks that were found on the wood road leading down to the Luther Evans bridge from the camp at the spring by the swamp on the mountain, near the spot where John Harbour met his untimely death. We should have found the hatchet that cut the sticks that formed the support for the coffee pot over the diminutive campfire whose smoke curling heavenward among the silent tree tops caught the eyes of the deer hunters, changed all their carefully

65

The family left behind: Widow Nettie Eddy Harbour and her four children. The older ones are Guy and Lura and the younger two are Polly and Amy. Dr. John R. Howard, who provided these photographs, is the son of Amy and her husband, Raymond E. Howard. *Courtesy of Dr. John R. Howard.*

prearranged plans and sent them in the night seven miles away across mountain streams, wooded hills, rocky defiles, and tangled underbrush—even miles of the hardest tramping found this side of the Cilkout [?] Pass. We should have been in on the Castle Meadows before those hunters came out of the mountains and had them conduct us back over the trail they said they took that dark and grewsome [sic] night—back to the scene of the tragedy. On the way back we should have stopped at the shanty and got the hatchet from the shelf over the entrance door where they said they left it, and where no living human being has since seen it, so far as can be ascertained, as though spirit hands had stretched forth and drawn it from hiding and hurled it hence into the impenetrable thickets, never again to be discovered of human eye. Once back at the scene of the shooting, we should have compared the shred of cloth found on the jagged rock with any torn garment that might be found near by, either cast aside or on human form; then we should have gone with the hunters to the little deserted camp at the spring and compared the nicks in the hatchet blade with the ribs on the sharpened crotch sticks that supported the coffee pail over the fire, and then come out over the Evans road for the purpose of making certain comparisons of footprints—the new with the old, for instance. And then we should have come down the valley to the humble home where lay at peace with all the world the victim of a bullet shot by the most cowardly hand that ever pulled the trigger of a gun—cowardly because the perpetrator of the deed dragged the victim of his error or design, hid it away from the sight of its dear ones and skulked under the cover of darkness from the mountain top and gave no sign. And then we and the hunters should have crossed the threshold of that devoted home where weeping children of a loved and loving sire bereft clung helplessly about a stricken mother widowed as by a bolt of lightning hurled from a cloudless sky; and into the death chamber we should have gone—we and the huntsmen—and paused beside the bier and looked upon the tranquil countenance, and in the solemn and impressive presence of the quick and the dead brought face to face taken note if the mute lips accused the guilty one. These things we should have done had we been the keen and shrewed and tireless sleuth that law should set upon the track of crime. But now the scent is cold. Until "thieves fall out and honest men receive their dues," we shall never know: Who KILLED John Harbour!

An epilogue of sorts appeared forty-one years later with the obituary of John Harbour's widow, Nettie Eddy Harbour, who died in June 1938 at the age of eighty-one. A notice in the *Bennington Banner* said:

The recent death of Mrs. John Harbour recalls the death of John Harbour in the woods of Pine Valley almost forty years ago. The case was most mysterious. Mr. Harbour was in the woods during the deer season with a party of Bennington hunters and was found dead a long distance from camp after he had failed to return at night. He had been killed instantly with a bullet through the head and the shooting was never explained. No one suspected for an instant that he had been murdered, but all believed the shooting was accidental and Mrs. Harbour had hoped for years that the hunter who fired the fatal shot would finally come forward and tell the story. He never has and thirty-eight years have now elapsed.

Chapter 7

THE BRIEF FLOWERING OF A SOUTH GLASTENBURY SUMMER RESORT

The years 1897–98, as noted, proved to be a time of great transition. Not only were the upland wilds of Glastenbury made familiar to the public by articles about the death of John Harbour, but it was also a time when operators of the old Bennington & Glastenbury Railroad, "the electric trolley," were stretching to recoup hard-to-generate dollars from their substantial investment. Obviously, ferners were not going to provide much revenue, but picnickers, sportsmen, fishermen or vacationing merchants plus their families—tourists from out of state seeking fresh air—now there's a possible idea that could be marketed!

Could an appealing business plan be devised that would take advantage of an upscale "summer resort" in clean mountain air? The old loggers' boardinghouse could become a "hotel," and the company store and apartments might be transformed into a "casino" or inn. Trout could be stocked in the streams for fishermen. Croquet, lawn tennis, tent platforms, hiking trails—it all had the makings of a romantically commercial idea.

Just which entrepreneurs were involved in the conversion of a mountainside logging community to a summer resort has never been clear. Logic suggests that the railroad owners were behind the scheme. One obscure reference to an investor is the name of Henry W. Martin of Bennington. But no other names, beyond that of Superintendent Sullivan of the trolley line, were ever identified with the project in several published news accounts.

One cannot help but wonder about the role of village scribe Henry Clay Day, who was a pharmacist in Bennington as well as the local correspondent for the *Troy Times*. After his death in 1919, Day left to posterity twenty-five volumes of local newspaper clippings, some of them copied in his own handwriting, plus his own handwritten notes, all of which now constitute a collection known as "the Day Papers." He began the scrapbooks about 1870 and kept them up until 1916.

The Day Papers have been available for many years to researchers in the library of the Bennington Museum, where an extensive name and subject index, compiled in the 1920s, facilitates access to the information. Recently, because of their fragility, the

The loggers' boardinghouse at South Glastenbury, with several residents posing for a photograph. Note the village schoolhouse at left, with a cupola. *Courtesy of Images from the Past.*

The casino at South Glastenbury in its prime, which narrows the time of this picture to 1897 or 1898.`

69

The old casino at South Glastenbury as it began to deteriorate after the "freshet of '98" washed out the trolley tracks and bridges. No image has ever been seen of a clock in that clock tower. *Courtesy of Images from the Past.*

original papers were placed in storage but they are available on microfilm, a set of which is also found in the Bennington Free Library's local history room.

Day's role in the attempted transformation of South Glastenbury is evident because he wrote articles about it as if he were personally promoting tourism in Glastenbury. He also left detailed notes about the renovation of the buildings, including costs and who did the work. Never once did he identify any persons who conceived the idea or who paid out goodly sums to restructure the logging village of South Glastenbury.

The old boardinghouse did become a hotel and clubhouse with a dance hall and dining room. The company store, dominated by a picturesque clock tower and located at the foot of a steep mountainside, became the Glastenbury Inn, to which fresh clams and oysters and all sorts of comestibles could be hauled via the railroad. A hatchery was stocked with thousands of trout.

Here is a sample of the favorable kind of "press" the proposed summer resort received. The article appeared under the headline "A Trout Hatchery at Glastenbury" in the *Bennington Banner* of September 14, 1897:

> *The Bennington and Woodford Electric Railway Company has begun the construction of a large trout hatchery at the terminus of the line in Glastenbury. Twelve large hatching boxes will be put in, and it is thought that at least 1,000,000 fry will be ready for the streams by another season.*

The lands around the clubhouse and hotel will be made attractive, and ample grounds for croquet and lawn tennis will be fitted up.

There is some talk of a new hotel, larger and more convenient than the old one, being built another season, though several cottages in place of a hotel may be decided upon.

This week six or seven well known New York physicians will arrive in Bennington and go to Glastenbury to look the place over, with the view of sending such patients as require a high altitude, really pure water and a bracing mountain air.

Note that the article provides no attribution and neglects quite deliberately to identify any entrepreneurs who were planning such grandiose improvements to a worn-out lumber camp. Newswriting practice, even of a century ago, would dictate that an important element of such a story would be to include names of financial backers of the project and their principal agents or spokesmen. But none of those elements are included. The article appears to have been written by someone on the inside. Suspicion necessarily points to the writer, Henry Clay Day, the pharmacist and inveterate newspaper clipper and sometime Bennington correspondent for the *Troy Times*.

Day also left a page of handwritten notes with details of the improvements to buildings at South Glastenbury, including what each item cost, for a grand total of $4,590. He described a two-story [saw]mill that was converted into a hotel, and said it measured 125 by 45 feet. "An entire new wall was put in with 95 piers," he wrote. He added these details:

1st story new floors, ceiled sides & overhead. Made into pool, bowling & billiard rooms below. 2nd story—all ceiled & finished in natural wood, a steward's room, victualling pantry, 3 servants' rooms and general restaurant. In the rear, upstairs, the front part is for dancing & opera hall 45 x 72 ft, 32 feet high.

There is a double veranda 137 feet long, 8 ft. wide, double veranda across west side 45 ft long. 50 new windows, 2 sets double doors leading to lowest veranda; 3 single doors leading out on veranda. A new roof, 4 dormer windows making it resemble 4 cottages.

The old hotel was given new underpinnings, with the lower story made into a reading room and offices, and a second, third and fourth story for family apartments and 20 rooms. "The lawn comprises 3 acres for croquet and tennis. Also 3 fish hatcherys." The icehouse at the casino, Day said, was 20 by 22 by 14 feet and would hold 130 tons of ice. He neglected to suggest from where all that ice would come—from lakes in winter and hauled up by rail?

A financial breakdown was provided: refitting the mill at $3,100; the hotel, $1,100; the walks, lawn, bridges, et cetera, $400; and icehouse at casino, $100. The bottom line of $4,590 was a sizeable outlay of cash in 1897, equivalent to well over $100,000 in early twenty-first-century terms. Figuring a 3 percent average yearly inflation, $4,590 in 1897 would approach $100,000 today; figuring at 4 percent, closer to $250,000.

The only names Day identified were those of Warren M. Freeman, who did the work, and J.L. Neice of Port Ewen, New York, who was the "inspector." This writer could not locate Freeman's name in Bennington region business or residential directories of the time.

Little or nothing else appeared in the newspaper—and nothing in the Day Papers—until the following summer; that singular summer of 1898, when it became clear that Day was perfecting his skills in public relations. Several small and tantalizing articles appeared in July and August. For example, on July 9 the *Banner* reported:

> *An excursion party of about one hundred came over on the trolley car from Hoosick Falls Thursday and went to Glastenbury, where they picnicked. A large part of them were members or descendants of the Sweet family, representatives being present from as far away as Ohio. The party had some mishaps on the trip, but all finally arrived at their destination and apparently had a good time.*

And then an absolutely euphoric account of the July doings at the north end of the railroad during its brief heyday appeared in the *Troy Daily Times*. Under the headline "Visitors at Glastenbury," *Times* correspondent Day rhapsodized about the invigorating "life in full midsummer swing" at the new popular resort at South Glastenbury. The same article, with minor changes, also appeared in the *Bennington Banner*:

> *Life is in full midsummer swing at Glastenbury, a popular resort at the terminus of the Bennington and Woodford electric railroad. The route from Bennington lays [sic] for nearly nine miles through a narrow winding valley that gradually trends in a northeasterly direction. A bright, clear stream courses the valley and the forests come down the steep hillsides to the stream.*
>
> *For several miles toward the terminus of the road there is not a human habitation in sight, nothing but vast mountains and interminable forests. To the stranger riding for the first time over the road the low buzzing of the trolley seems a great novelty in these vast forest-clad domains. On every bright, warm afternoon the cars of the company are well filled with ladies, summer visitors and others, who are simply enjoying a trolley ride or who are in search of a few hours of restful quiet among the mountains.*
>
> *The car does some hard climbing between Bennington and Glastenbury, finally reaching a height of about 2,000 feet above the former place. On the return trip the trolley is usually detached from the overhead wire and the car descends into Bennington by mere gravity alone.*
>
> *At Glastenbury there are two buildings standing at the junction of two valleys, one of which runs to the east and the other to the northwest. One of the buildings is the large clubhouse, dancing hall and dining room of the company all combined under one roof, and the other is the Glastenbury Inn, which is designed simply for lodgers. Just at present berrying and fishing parties are frequent visitors to the various sections along the line. Strawberries are still found in the narrow shaded valley at Glastenbury.*
>
> *Last week was almost a record breaker in the number of good sized parties that visited Glastenbury and partook of a trout dinner at the clubhouse. State Auditor Hale and a party of lawyers, Rev. W.H. Pimm and party, of Babylon, Long Island, and W.H. Bradford and party [of Bennington] were among the larger gatherings.*
>
> *William Winslow, the Main Street hardware dealer, is encamped for a couple of weeks a short distance below the hotel. The Stars and Stripes are floating from his canvas*

abode and William's stalwart and familiar figure is generally in full view from every passing car. His little camp is close by a crystal stream and embowered in trees dark with leafy shade.

All through the section little parties are encamped, some for only two or three days and some for two or three weeks. Just above the Winslow camp a French artist sat for three days last week on a big rock in the middle of the stream, sketching his clubhouse, the inn and the grand sweep of mountain scenery.

Through the courtesy of Superintendent Sullivan the members of the press in Bennington were given a free ride and a trout dinner at Glastenbury Saturday afternoon. The dinner consisted of several courses and every moment of the visit of the newspaper men was thoroughly enjoyed. The flow of good spirits was kept up from start to finish. The little party broke up at the close of the day, stopping on the way home for a short visit to Editor Livingston of The Reformer *at his summer cottage at Ferndale.*

So much for an enthusiastic newspaper article from the *Troy Daily Times* of July 1898 about the heyday of the summer resort that flowered so briefly in South Glastenbury. But there was more. On July 26 under a headline of "Trout and Scenery/Newspaper Representatives Entertained at Glastenbury Inn," the news media admitted having been co-opted:

Last Saturday afternoon Superintendent Sullivan of the Bennington & Woodford railroad entertained local representatives of the press with a trout dinner at the Glastenbury Inn. It was a meal to be remembered, comprising, besides the gamy fish, which formed the chief feature, an abundance, in fact a superabundance, of other good things artistically cooked neatly served and much enjoyed by the guests. Mr. Sullivan is doing everything in his power to make this resort attractive and a large and growing patronage shows that his efforts are being appreciated. The inn is a refreshing refuge from the heat and bustle of the village, and the ride up, one of the most picturesque possible.

An hour spent over cigars and in informal chat formed a fitting final to a pleasant visit and the party in due season took the cars for home, stopping on the way to enjoy the hospitality of Editor Livingston's Ferndale cottage. Altogether it was a delightful trip.

Editor Livingston was our verbose friend from Chapter 6, James H. Livingston of the *Bennington Reformer*.

And on August 9:

The Masonic lodges of Bennington, North Bennington and Arlington, together with Eastern Star chapters, are picnicking at Glastenbury today. The out-of-town people came down on the early train. There is [sic] a good number of them and they went prepared to have a good time. The hotel at that point has all the boarders that it can accommodate. Travel to that point and Hoosick Falls was brisk Sunday, the cars being filled every trip.

A classic view of the one-season (1898) South Glastenbury summer resort, with children crossing a bridge over Bolles Brook and new customers emerging from the electric trolley from Bennington. The hotel, *at left,* had been a boardinghouse for loggers converted to a hotel, and the casino, *right,* was the old company store and apartments. *Courtesy of Dr. John R Howard.*

And on August 12:

> *There was a large attendance at the Masonic picnic given at Glastenbury Tuesday. Parties were present from Arlington, North Bennington and here. The trip by the electric car up the mountains was all that one could want. The women of Mt. Anthony chapter O.E.S., assumed the principal charge of the affair. The High School orchestra was present during the day and rendered the music.*

The backers of this wondrous seasonal spa, who were never made public, clearly had the sophistication to take advantage of newspaper publicity. The piece in the *Troy Times* reads as if it were planted and paid for. It would stand to reason that the owners of the railroad were principal backers of the resort concept, but the flowing articles written without attribution by Henry Clay Day suggest that he had much to do with it. Upon his death in 1919, the obituary offered no clues.

At the end of that one season of 1898, the effort to market Glastenbury as a trolley-equipped summer haven for French artists, wealthy doctors from Long Island, parties of vacationing lawyers and accountants, tenting Main Street merchants, necktie-clad

Glastenbury !

BENNINGTON & WOODFORD ELECTRIC R. R.

WILL OPEN

SATURDAY, JULY 16,

And run to Glastenbury. First car leaving North St. at 9 A.M. and every forty-five minutes thereafter until 8:15 P.M. Returning from Glastenbury, first car at 9:45 A.M. and last car at 10 P.M.

Meals, on order, will be served at Pavillion at any time. Regular dinner from 12 to 3 P.M. at 75c. Trout dinner at $1.00. Orders can be given the day previous for large parties.

GLASTENBURY INN is also open. Well furnished rooms and first-class table will be provided to parties desiring board. For terms apply to management.

GLASTENBURY INN,

Bennington = = = = Vt.

This enticement for tourists and summer visitors was published in July 1898 in the weekly *Bennington Banner*.

fishermen and croquet fanciers came to a crashing disaster when floodwaters washed out the tracks beyond repair. It was called "the freshet of '98" as it remained in the memory banks of Benningtonians. No acknowledgement seemed to be given to the fact that a clear-cut forest is especially susceptible to erosion and flooding. The newly renovated buildings were abandoned and allowed to deteriorate back into the compost of forest floor. A fortune had been spent on the place, but now there was no longer any way to get there!

Today, the old right of way can be hiked as it snakes its way out of Bennington, passing near former ochre beds and iron ore pits before it passes the crumbling nineteenth-century furnace stacks at Furnace Grove near the Bennington-Woodford line. Mixed in the track bed are shiny bits of slag, byproducts of the furnace. Scattered along the trail are evidences of charcoal and red bricks, clues to whereabouts of the kilns. The tracks themselves were pulled up for World War II scrap metal—giving Glastenbury the highest per capita scrap total in all of Vermont. Occasional spikes or rusty plates lie about in the underbrush.

All these artifacts offer a laboratory for the study of a short-lived, labor-intensive technology that flourished for a couple of decades in this high-elevation neighborhood of the Green Mountains.

Glastenbury's decline virtually coincided with the launching of the twentieth century. The little community of South Glastenbury, which began as a logging settlement, once had a post office, a school and several small houses, then aspired to upgrade to a summer resort and was wiped out by a flood, never to recover. As Woodford old-timer Truman Mallary recounted in the 1930s, "The freshet of that year [1898] destroyed many of the bridges and so much of the road that it was never replaced."

The concept of a summer resort had been chancy to start with and probably would not have paid off for many seasons, if ever. To have the whole enterprise made inaccessible by a flood after its first season was a serious loss—to someone. Fortunately for posterity, some excellent photographs were taken of tourists riding the trolleys, and of fishermen testing the waters of Bolles Brook, with the Glastenbury Inn and picturesque clock tower in the background. If those pictures did not exist, it would be difficult to believe that this commercial activity had ever occured.

Chapter 8

DECLINE, DISINCORPORATION AND DISAPPEARANCE

By virtue of the fact that every town in Vermont, regardless of population, was entitled to one member of the House of Representatives, Glastenbury was plugged in to statewide politics. And the record of its representation, according to the authoritative Deming's *Vermont Civil Officers*, shows that no year was omitted starting with the town's organization in 1834, when Mark Hotchkiss was elected. For the years 1835 to 1841, Asa G. Hewes, son of Dr. Elijah Hewes, represented the town. Then a series of musical chairs seems to have been played until 1870 as John Elwell Sr. and Jr. exchanged the office several times, as did John H. Mattison, William McDonald, Jeremiah McDonald and others named Ishmael R. Elwell, William Stockwell, George Eddy and Charles Barton.

The year 1870 became a dividing point in Vermont politics because a constitutional change doubled the term of office for principal state officials as well as legislators from one year to two—which it remains to this day. In the years after 1872 until 1900 the office of legislator in Glastenbury went to persons named Mattison seven times, along with others named Truman T. Elwell, Daniel Romaine, Obed Eddy, Trenor P. Harbour, German E. Harrington, Edgar Green, Hugh E. Cone and Robert B. Young.

At the turn of the twentieth century, with South Glastenbury having no residents, only tiny Fayville remained inhabited, and that was only accessible by road through Shaftsbury. Through the early years of the twentieth century, the population of Glastenbury and its neighbor to the east, Somerset, dwindled toward single digits. In 1920, census enumerators counted seventeen persons in Glastenbury, several of whom were listed as boarders; in other words, transient loggers. A decade later at the dawn of the Great Depression, the number was down to seven, consisting of five Mattisons and two Hazards. Over in Somerset, accessible by vehicle on a ten-mile gravel road from Route 9, the Molly Stark Trail, at Searsburg, the 1930 census counted twenty persons, mostly named Taylor, several of whom were children.

In the early years of the century, two of Glastenbury's legislators were Robert Brigham Young and John L. Mattison. Young was born in 1864 in Burke, New York, settled in

Glastenbury in 1888 and served in the Vermont House in 1898 and again in 1912. His occupation was listed as farmer, and he also served as Glastenbury's treasurer, lister, road commissioner and a justice. The 1920 census listed Young as a fifty-five-year-old servant of Aurilla Mattison. John Mattison, born in 1890, served in the House in 1925, and was a member of its committees on land taxes and temperance. Also a farmer, he was a Glastenbury selectman, school director, lister and second constable.

The fact that so very few citizens held all municipal offices in these two towns began to stir concern in political circles statewide. The syndicated cartoon feature *Believe It or Not* by Ripley published a sketch in the mid-1930s of a man and two women with the amazing caption: "The Mattison family is the whole town of Glastenbury, Vt. Ira Mattison and his wife and his mother hold every town office."

The two legislators from Glastenbury and Somerset held vastly disproportionate power in Montpelier, and this situation began to irritate the larger towns. Vermont may be a state of small towns, but these two were of particularly minuscule size. Glastenbury's legislator carried the same weight as his counterpart in Burlington, Rutland or any other city or town. In places like Bennington, Brattleboro, Barre, Montpelier or Newport, political figures were becoming aware that a ridiculous situation was developing as the gap widened between large and small towns.

The many other small towns were more cautious, of course. If the autonomy of a town of 7 or 20 could be threatened, then a town of 44 or 73 might ask: Where is the line going to be drawn? The legislature was the only place where such inequities could be remedied, but it was dominated by the many small towns. That is why nothing happened until, ultimately, a much more powerful authority, the U.S. Supreme Court, leveraged the change. And that did not happen until 1965 when the Vermont House was reapportioned and—with a federal gun to its head—arranged to downsize from 246 to 150.

Nonetheless, during the disincorporation drama of 1937, Glastenbury's status became completely linked in the public mind with Somerset's because of all the news media attention. During 1937 the Taylor family of Somerset gained notoriety not only because of rampant rumors of "corrupt one-family rule," but also because criminal charges were brought against John H. Taylor for abusing his foster children. From her pulpit as legislator, Representative Katie E. Taylor publicly protested disincorporation, but there seemed little she could defend against because newspapers kept focusing on the Somerset scandal.

In Glastenbury, Representative Ira H. Mattison never attended the 1937 session of the legislature. Yet he was able to travel to New York City in 1936 to be interviewed on the radio version of Ripley's *Believe it or Not*. The conversation involved that year's election and Franklin D. Roosevelt's landslide victory over Governor Alf Landon of Kansas. It was this election that gave popularity to the phrase "As goes Vermont, so goes Maine" because those were the only states to support Landon.

Glastenbury's three votes were cast for Roosevelt, naturally, because the Mattisons had earned a reputation as Democrats in this state—a state that, at that time, boasted the largest faction of Republicans of all the American states. Secrecy of the ballot booth

BELIEVE IT OR NOT! (Reg. U. S. Patent Office.) *By Ripley*

CHAS. FRANCIS ADAMS - Secretary of the Navy
A MEMBER OF THE ADAMS FAMILY, WHICH HAS BEEN IN POLITICS EVER SINCE JOHN ADAMS

THE *HOMING PIGEON* TOOK OFF FROM BOWMAN FIELD, FLEW DUE SOUTH FOR HALF AN HOUR AND LANDED ON THE SPOT FROM WHICH IT TOOK OFF!

REASON? WIND VELOCITY.

© 1932 King Features Syndicate, Inc., Great Britain rights reserved.

DRAWN BY JACK HARRIS AGE 12

THE HORSESHOE TREE
IN LEECHVILLE, N.C.

THE MATTISON FAMILY
IS THE WHOLE TOWN OF GLASTENBURY, Vt.
IRA MATTISON AND HIS WIFE AND HIS MOTHER HOLD EVERY TOWN OFFICE. Rip.

A PIG WITH 2 SNOUTS AND 2 MOUTHS
Owned by MRS. J.A LAURENCE
-Newburyport, Mass.

3-18

EXPLANATION OF YESTERDAY'S CARTOON
ALL ITEMS SELF-EXPLANATORY

A nationally syndicated newspaper feature publicized the one-family nature of Glastenbury in 1936.

may be sacred, but in a town of three voters it was known that the Democratic votes were cast by Ira, his wife Louise and his mother Angelia. (The 1930 census listed Aurilla Mattison, age seventy-three, as head of the family, whereas Angelia A. Mattison, age seventy-one, was listed as "mother." Both were noted to be widowed. The only non-Mattison in the 1930 census was Charles A. Williams, age eighteen and a cousin.)

When Ripley's *Believe It or Not* cartoon depicted the trio with the words, "Ira Mattison and his wife and his mother hold every town office," it approached the truth but did not tell the whole truth. The *Vermont Yearbook* for 1936, the final full year of existence for Glastenbury, lists the town's municipal data this way:

GLASTENBURY (B-10), BENNINGTON CO.—*Pop. 7. Area, 27,341 acres. R.R. from South Shaftsbury. Tax Rate—$2.40. Grand List—$639.52.*

OFFICERS *(p.o. South Shaftsbury)—Clerk, I.N. Mattison; Treas., Louise M. Mattison; Auditors, I.N. Mattison, Caroline Hazard, Rowland Hazard; Selectmen, I.N. Mattison, Rowland Hazard, A. A. Mattison; Constable, A.A. Mattison; Listers, I.N. Mattison, L.M. Mattison, Rowland Hazard; Road Commissioner, I.N. Mattison; School Directors, Rowland Hazard, L.M. Mattison, A.A. Mattison; Overseer, Selectmen; Agent, Rowland Hazard; Grand Juror, I.N. Mattison; Tax Collector, Louise Mattison; Fire Warden, I.N. Mattison; Health Officer, I.N. Mattison; Justices, Caroline Hazard, Rowland Hazard, A.A. Mattison; Supt. of Schools, F.S. Irons, Bennington. Merchant, Norman Mattison Est.*

Rowland Hazard first appeared as a town official in the 1935 *Vermont Yearbook*, and in 1936, as seen above, was joined by Caroline Hazard. In 1937 because of the legislature's action, Glastenbury had no entry in the *Yearbook*.

Rowland Hazard was a fascinating figure—a wealthy tenth-generation Rhode Islander and an aggressive political and entrepreneurial figure in the strongest American capitalist tradition—whose life was plagued by incurable alcoholism. In 1929 he and his wife, Helen Hamilton Campbell, were divorced, and they remarried in 1931 before taking a lengthy summer tour of Europe. Caroline was their daughter. It is a mystery as to why Rowland and Caroline Hazard held the only public offices in Glastenbury with Ira Mattison and his wife and mother. Around 1930 Hazard built his summer home, Sugarbush, on an old cellar hole foundation at the junction of the Glastenbury Road and the road to Fayville—it was one of several residences he owned. His other homes were in Shaftsbury, Manhattan and New Mexico. Hazard also had ancestral homes in Peace Dale and Narragansett, Rhode Island. (The village of Peace Dale in the town of South Kingstown was named for his ancestors whose surname was Peace.) While in Switzerland in 1931, Hazard famously sought the counsel of the psychiatrist Carl Jung to try to cure his alcoholism. More will be told about Rowland Hazard in Chapter 9, which discusses the acquisition of the Hazard property by Dr. Richard Sterba, who had his own close connections with another international giant of psychiatry, Sigmund Freud.

Some hints as to the nature of the reputation of a town ruled by one family can be seen in Glastenbury's town records, in old leather-bound ledger books in the vault of the Bennington County clerk, who keeps official records of any unorganized towns or gores in the county. The treasurer's ledger, for instance, which runs from 1899 to 1936, bulges with evidence of cash payments made to Ira N., Aurilla and Angelia Mattison. Ira, who was selectman, treasurer and road commissioner, among several other elected and appointed positions, paid himself for working on the town roads, school purposes (there was no school then) and bobcat bounties. The one-time economic importance of ferning is indicated by an agreement on file in town records by which Glastenbury farmer Robert B. Young paid one hundred dollars for the right to pick ferns on all lands owned by Hall Park McCullough, a prominent lawyer in New York City and North Bennington who, as will be seen, collected parcels of Glastenbury land as a kind of hobby.

Statewide, much of the 1937 disincorporation drama was played out in the pages of the *Burlington Free Press* and *Rutland Herald*, then the state's only morning dailies. Both papers frequently published comment or editorials from other papers, and gave prominent attention to Somerset's foster child abuse scandal.

Ira Mattison may have been on the radio in New York and depicted in a nationally syndicated newspaper feature, but he was never heard from statewide. He burnished his isolated image by neglecting even to take his oath of office for the 1937 legislative session. He did not appear at all in Montpelier, a fact that tended to trivialize any claims he might have made regarding the seriousness with which a town of seven inhabitants could conduct business. Ira's reputation as "dictator" of one of these single-family towns—justified or not—was never rebutted.

Curiously, the daily newspaper nearest to Glastenbury paid little attention to this issue that attracted such interest elsewhere in Vermont, an issue that focused on a weak link in the state's constitutional structure. Other than one front-page item on March 26, which reported that bills to disincorporate had been introduced, the *Bennington Banner* carried virtually nothing until an editorial comment on the last day of the year, December 31, marked the official demise of the town.

Other Vermont newspapers carried plenty of ammunition. On March 12, 1937, articles appeared in both the *Herald* and *Free Press* reporting that John H. Taylor of Somerset had been arrested and charged with unnecessary cruelty to his two adopted children, Theodore and Carl Taylor, ages fifteen and seventeen. Taylor was owner of Somerset's principal farm and was Representative Katie E. Taylor's husband.

The headlines read, "Husband of Somerset Representative Arrested on Accusations of Cruelty to Two Youngsters" and "Somerset Man, Whose Wife Is Legislator, Said to Have Beaten Two Boys." According to charges filed by the Windham County state's attorney, Taylor had worked the boys from 4:00 a.m. to 10:00 p.m. seven days a week, beaten them with his fists, a strap, a pitchfork and an axe handle and had cursed them and failed to provide them with proper winter clothing. The article added, "Taylor's wife is serving her seventh consecutive term as representative in the Legislature...Somerset has a population of less than 10."

The next day the *Free Press* headline read, "Taylor Laughing at Arraignment in Cruelty Case." The story contained little to justify those words except the final sentence: "Taylor smiled broadly when that part of the warrants charging he struck the boys with fists, strap, pitchfork and axe handle was read."

On March 26, the bills were introduced in the legislature to declare the towns of Somerset and Glastenbury unorganized, followed by the first test of political sentiment on March 29, when the Senate ordered, on a roll call vote of twenty-four to two, the advance of the bill to a third reading. The roll call was requested by Representative Taylor.

At an April 2 hearing only one person spoke, and that was to oppose the Somerset-Glastenbury bill. Attorney Deane C. Davis of Barre contended that reasons for disincorporating these two towns could be applied with equal validity to nearly one hundred other Vermont towns. News accounts did not specify whether Davis spoke for a client or on his own. (Later, Davis was twice elected governor of Vermont.)

The legislative issue was debated in an atmosphere of consistently skeptical newspaper attention. A *Burlington Free Press* editorial on March 10 favored disincorporation but expressed these wry doubts:

> *At last the Vermont Legislature is making an effort to do something about the status of towns which have been reduced to one family and in which that single family "runs the town," collected taxes (largely from power companies or non-residents who own land there) and have full control of expenditures. That such conditions should exist, and that these one-family towns should have equal representation in the lower House of the Legislature with cities having thousands of people is so absurd that it probably would be impossible in any other state unless it might be New Hampshire. Whether the House will have sufficient courage to cut down its own membership, however, remains to be seen. It will be almost a miracle if it happens.*

Reference to the power company meant the New England Power (NEPCO) that in 1912 built the Somerset Dam as the starting point of an ambitious hydroelectric power generating facility that tapped the dramatic drop in elevation of the Deerfield River. NEPCO did indeed own and pay taxes on the dam and substantial landholdings in Somerset, as well as lands through which the hydrosystem flowed in Searsburg, Wilmington and Whitingham, and to a generating plant in Readsboro. Completion of the massive so-called Davis Bridge dam in 1923 created the largest body of water completely within Vermont's borders, called Lake Whitingham. Later, that dam and the lake were renamed for civil engineer Henry I. Harriman who conceptualized the power generating complex, which extends into Massachusetts.

The *Bennington Banner*'s only article of substance during 1937 appeared March 9 under the headline "Would Remove Towns' Rights," here offered verbatim:

> *The name of Mattison dominates the town of Glastenbury in Bennington County. This town of 7 inhabitants, has a larger area than Somerset, 27,341 acres. The grand list*

for 1936 was fixed at $636.60 and with a tax rate of $2.40, thus giving a tax yield per year of $1,527.84.

Ira N. Mattison, the head of the town, gained a modicum of publicity recently by not showing up at the 1937 session of the Legislature as the elected representative from Glastenbury. Two years ago, he was nearly two months late in making his appearance.

A long distance away, on the Canadian border, the *Newport Express* had kept up a drumbeat of criticism, and its editorials were reprinted in other papers. On March 10, the same day as the *Free Press* editorial, these comments from Newport also appeared in the *Free Press*:

Perhaps the Somerset incident into which Mrs. Katie Taylor's name has been drawn will show how easily it is for one-family towns to feather their own nests and will lead to some simple legislation which will force a town back into an unorganized state when its population has fallen below a certain fixed figure.

We have all the machinery for conducting the business of such towns and there is no reason why such town organizations as Somerset and Glastenbury should continue to exist. It is not too late for the present Legislature to act.

On March 10 an influential editorial appeared in the *Rutland Herald*, undoubtedly written by Robert W. Mitchell, then earning a solid reputation as Montpelier correspondent for the Vermont Press Bureau, an awkward alliance of the *Herald* and *Free Press* for purposes of sharing statewide coverage. Mitchell later became the *Herald*'s publisher, a position he held until his death in 1993. He became known for editorials often more devoted to information and cogitation than to persuasion. This was an example:

The towns of Glastenbury and Somerset have lately attracted a good deal of attention, both because of their infinitesimal size and the doings of their "first families."

Now it is proposed to introduce a bill in the Legislature to unorganize the two towns and put their administration in the hands of a county supervisor.

It is not likely that this move will be appreciated by the Mattisons of Glastenbury and the Taylors of Somerset. In the latter town, the big thing is the power company's dam which is supposed to pay most of the town's taxes and the Taylors hold between them 10 or more of the town's offices. Somerset has a grand list of $5,548.97, a tax rate of $1, so the revenues are not excessive, practically all administered by the Taylor family. There does not seem to be very much wrong with this picture except that Mrs. Taylor, representing 20 people or less, elected by perhaps six voters, has as much say and as many votes as the city of Burlington, and the representative from Glastenbury, when and if he appears in Montpelier, can offset the vote of the city of Rutland.

There are at least a dozen other towns that do not poll a great many votes yet have full representation in the House. Baltimore with 27 votes, Stratton with 21, Brunswick with 32, Landgrove with 34, St. George with 35, Brookline with 41, East Haven with 43, for example. Nobody can defend as fair and equitable this survival of the ancient system of township representation, provided when all towns were more or less alike, but a good many champions will be found for the small-vote towns when it comes to the pinch.

Two days later the *Herald* published this brief and pointless editorial comment it attributed to the *Bennington Banner*:

We need some concentrations in Vermont. There are said to be plenty of folks at the state house who would like to annex Glastenbury to Shaftsbury and Somerset to Searsburg, but it isn't likely to happen.

That date, March 12, was also when the news reports disclosed the criminal charges against John Taylor. On April 8, the following news item appeared—in its entirety—in the *Herald* under the headline "Bills to Disorganize 2 Towns Advanced to Third Reading":

MONTPELIER, April 7.—The House of Representatives advanced to third and final reading this afternoon two bills making Somerset and Glastenbury unorganized towns despite vigorous denials of Mrs. Katie E. Taylor, representative from Somerset, that her town is run by one family. After the Somerset bill was advanced on a roll call, 138 to 52, the Glastenbury bill was quickly disposed of.

Representative [Walter] Hard of Manchester gave chief impetus to passage of the Somerset bill with the statement, "It's a self-evident proposition that where in short one family runs the town we have not democracy but we have oligarchy."

Both bills were amended so that provisions revoking their charters were omitted. Provisions that the towns should cease to exist as municipal corporations remained in the bill.

The changes were recommended by the committee on municipal corporations after questions had been raised on the constitutional right of the Legislature to revoke a charter given by another state, New Hampshire, and on the safety of property rights in the town.

Mrs. Taylor said she had heard the bill relating to her town was framed to stop a "racket." She denied existence of any racket and explained that the town had "taken money for roads." Taxes on power company holdings are said to constitute a large part of the revenue of the thinly populated town.

For reasons that escape logic today, editorial comment in the *Bennington Banner* about the disincorporation of Glastenbury waited until the final day of the milestone year of 1937. Though unsigned, it is clear that the following was written by the *Banner*'s publisher, Frank E. "Ginger" Howe, because the writer identifies himself in the context:

At the close of business tonight [Dec. 31] Vermont has 246 towns instead of 248 which was the correct number this morning.

Glastenbury has been a town for about a hundred years, being organized, we believe, in 1834, though it never had enough people to warrant a town charter. The most votes this writer can remember being cast in Glastenbury in the 36 years he has been a resident of the county was eleven, and in recent years it has been down as low as three. There is very little tillable land in the township and Glastenbury should, probably, eventually become a part of the National Forest.

In trying to look up a little history of Glastenbury and Somerset, the writer found in the Beers, Ellis & Soule Gazetteer, *printed in 1868, a few lines about Glastenbury in which it was stated that "the town has eleven voters and every year votes unanimously Democratic."*

Glastenbury tried many years ago to join up with Shaftsbury but Shaftsbury refused, and seems to have done so without sufficient reason. Perhaps the Republicans living on the Shaftsbury plains didn't want those eleven solid Democratic votes joining with Pitt Montgomery's column marching down from Maple Hill.

In 1938 the *Banner* made up for its inattention to Glastenbury by publishing, in several installments, a series of chatty, historically flavored articles written by Rose Lindley Kent of Dorset. Most dealt with the incorporation of the Glastenbury Plank Road Company and the railroads.

The legislation of 1937 places most government functions in the hands of one county official, appointed by the governor, called supervisor of unorganized towns and gores. This official holds the powers of the board of selectmen, school board, constable, treasurer, auditor, town agent and most other offices rolled into one. To keep property assessments separate, a board of listers was created.

A year and a half after his town died, so did Ira N. Mattison. He was only forty-five, and had lived in the town all his life. On June 2, 1939, the *Banner* carried his obituary on the front page, as was its custom for prominent persons. It read:

He was of a retiring disposition but was generally liked by those who came to know him intimately, and a large number of friends will learn of his death with regret and will sympathize with the members of his family in their affliction.

Ira's mother died in 1941.

Ira's widow, Louise May Dunham Mattison, then moved into Bennington with her two sons, Roy, age seventeen, and James, age ten, leaving Glastenbury with an official population (in 1950) of one.

Roy Mattison, seventy-eight years old when this was written, resided with his wife Beaulah on the North Road in Shaftsbury and had fond recollections of his upbringing in Glastenbury. He showed this writer a snapshot of himself at about age four posing with a large bear Ira had shot. Because the town had no school, Roy attended the old Maple Hill School in Shaftsbury and remembered that the teacher was Laura Montgomery. His father had to pay the tuition to Shaftsbury, he said.

Mattison remembered many details such as precise dates of when members of his family died. What he did not remember was why his father declined to attend that session of the legislature in 1937 when Glastenbury reached the end of the Mattison era. The obituary said the reason was his mother's illness.

Members of the family of brothers J. Oliver Burt and Sidney A. Burt of Bennington enjoy an 1899 outing in Glastenbury on the ruins of the railroad that had washed out the year before. *Courtesy of Ruth Burt Ekstrom.*

After the departure of Ira Mattison's family, Glastenbury was left to the perpetrators of ghost town legends. If you Google the words "Bennington Triangle" or "Glastenbury Mountain," you will unearth verbiage that claims that as many as ten people have disappeared in undefined places that have some connection with or relevance to Glastenbury Mountain, and that phenomena described as supernatural, paranormal, weird, extraterrestrial, psychic or otherwise unexplained have been at work in this part of the world. Almost all of this is undocumented nonsense and serves to enhance the royalties of writers who put out books with titles like *Cursed in New England: Stories of Damned Yankees* or *Green Mountain Ghosts, Ghouls & Unsolved Mysteries*. Such legends commonly follow enormous tracts of lands such as the New Jersey Pine Barrens or the vast, unorganized townships of northern Maine.

Tales of strange happenings in the forests of Glastenbury are not new. Under a headline "Local Jottings" in the Bennington Banner of May 23, 1867, accounts of a "wild man" were reported:

> *For some days rumors have been rife of a "wild man" hereabouts, who during the daytime remains concealed for the most part in his lair, but when the "somber shades of eve" steal over the land, sallies out to his work of rascality, chasing lone women, and the like. At sundry times it is said he has made indecent exposures of his person to persons who have accidentally stumbled upon his rendezvous. More than this, it is claimed the fellow is armed with three revolvers, and carries a formidable looking dirk, joined to which he has an ugly phiz. All these reports may be exaggerated, and doubtless are, but still there can be no doubt that there is a man around here who has a failing in the line of chasing females, and peaking [sic] into windows at night. He may be a rascal intentionally, and he may be nothing more nor less than an escaped lunatic. But one thing is certain: a reign of terror has been inaugurated among our female population, making them exceedingly "scarry" about being out alone after night-fall. Our authorities should at once take measures to hunt out the fellow.*

A follow-up two weeks later reported that the wild man had been "cotched" and sent out of town. "He was tinged with a species of lunacy."

Glastenbury's supervisor today, Rickey Harrington, has picked up on the wild man, or "bigfoot," legend and incorporated it into his letterhead, making a sort of permanent and official tradition out of the town's supernatural reputation.

The only documented instance of a person who disappeared in the town of Glastenbury involved a seventy-four-year-old experienced hunter and fisherman named Middie Rivers, who vanished in the vast Bickford Hollow region on the opening weekend of deer season in November 1945. It was a case of genuine disappearance that is worth summarizing here but not for reasons of associating it with weird or supernatural conspiracy. When Rivers had not returned to the Lauzon camp on Monday after that opening weekend of deer season, his companions went into Bennington and asked Fire Chief Wallace Mattison to organize a search. Why the fire chief had jurisdiction in another town was not questioned, nor was there any suggestion in the newspaper that the county sheriff or other authorities should be involved.

The next day a group of fifteen of Rivers's coworkers from the BenMont Papers plant joined the search. When they had no luck, Chief Mattison put out a call for five hundred men to enter the forests of Glastenbury, and that number was publicized in large headline type on the front page of the Banner. But when his plea yielded only forty volunteers, the Bennington Board of Selectmen offered to pay four dollars to any person who would search for Middie Rivers. Finally, some soldiers from Fort Devens in Massachusetts were called upon. But after days with no clues of any kind, the search for the missing man slipped from the front pages and gradually became legend. In all the years since, hunters, hikers, fishermen and loggers have combed every square inch of Glastenbury and no sign of Middie Rivers has been located. A most plausible guess is that a hunter accidentally shot him, as happened to John Harbour in 1897, but in this case all evidence was carefully buried.

The ghostly legend was greatly enhanced just a year later by the disappearance of Bennington College student Paula Welden, who implausibly set out for a late afternoon hike on the Long Trail in Woodford on December 1, 1946. Many articles have been written—usually on an anniversary—about this girl's unsolved disappearance. The central fact is that no evidence of her, alive or dead, has ever emerged. Like Middie Rivers, she simply vanished.

Though Paula Welden was last seen walking toward dusk up the Long Trail Road, known now as Harbour Road, in Woodford, there is no evidence that she ever set foot in the town of Glastenbury, whose unmarked border is nearly a mile from where she was last seen. Yet several writers over the years have stretched the facts to fit the supernatural ghost town scenario.

One positive outcome of the Welden case was the formal organization of the Vermont State Police, which evolved in direct response to the lack of a central authority in charge of a coherent or professional investigation.

One of the man-made cairns on top of Glastenbury Mountain, the sixth highest summit in Vermont. Dave Lacy, the Forest Service archaeologist who took the photo, agrees it is mysterious but does not speculate on who might have assembled these rocks.

The search had fallen into the lap of Sheriff Clyde Peck, who was serving out lame duck tenure after having been defeated at the polls the previous November.

Paula Welden's father, W. Archibald Welden, a prominent businessman from Stamford, Connecticut, proved to be a dominant and even overbearing personality in the search. He attempted to organize his own search when the efforts of a state investigator named Almo Franzoni proved ineffectual, and he was critical of everyone, including the students from Bennington and Williams Colleges who volunteered to search, as well as President Lewis Webster Jones of Bennington College. News media from out of state focused on his complaints, feeding the aura of mystery and helping to create the negative reputation that led directly to the organization of a professional Vermont State Police force.

A history of difficult relations between Paula and her father led to speculation that her disappearance had been perhaps carefully planned to remove herself from an unhappy domestic situation. One theory—as unproven as any other—has always been that there was a rendezvous with a boyfriend who met her in a car and took her away to begin a new life somewhere. This notion at least fits the fact of a total lack of evidence.

It is surprising that the perpetrators of occult legends have not picked up on the similar reputation of Glastonbury, England, a place surrounded by myths that deal with the Holy Grail, the Holy Thorn and King Arthur. Glastonbury today attracts religious tourism and pilgrimages that involve diverse strains of mysticism and paganism.

Another Glastenbury (Vermont) mystery that the ghost and ghoul set has overlooked can be found at the very summit of the mountain in the form of three man-made stone cairns. These stone structures are truly mysterious. There are virtually no rocks elsewhere on the mountaintop, so the cairn components had to have been carried uphill for some distance.

Other stone cairns in Vermont have been identified by Princeton Professor Norman E. Muller, who has documented and photographed them in Rochester and Stockbridge in Windsor County, and Newfane in Windham County. Other examples have been found in Rhode Island, Pennsylvania and Connecticut.

Dave Lacy, archaeologist for the Green Mountain National Forest, provided a photograph of one of the Glastenbury summit cairns but declined to offer a theory other than to acknowledge that they are mysterious.

Chapter 9

A PARCEL COLLECTOR AND THE VIENNESE EQUESTRIAN INFLUENCE

Mention has been made of the Glastenbury landholdings of Trenor W. Park, the Woodford native who made a huge fortune after the gold rush days in California. Indeed, it was probably the largest fortune—factoring in inflation—ever made by a Vermonter. Park returned to the East Coast in 1865 to build the North Bennington mansion now known as the Park-McCullough House. He was elected to the Vermont legislature, engaged in often litigious involvement in railroads, sold the Panama Railroad at enormous profit to the French government at an auspicious time and died unexpectedly in 1882 at the age of fifty-nine. Park's life is an unparalleled saga of nineteenth-century aggressiveness, acquisitiveness and audacity. But the focus of this chapter is on the McCullough side of the equation.

The relationship between these men might best be understood if one remembers that Trenor Park was Vermont Governor Hiland Hall's son-in-law, and father-in-law to Vermont Governor John G. McCullough. The Glastenbury heritage of Trenor Park was carried on in a curious way by Park's grandson, who bore all three prominent family names: Hall Park McCullough.

Born in San Francisco in 1872, H.P. McCullough lived most of his long life in the old Hall farmhouse next to the mansion Park built. Today that farmhouse has been expanded and divided into attractive apartments dominated by a mammoth oak tree. H.P. McCullough, besides being the son of a governor (elected to one term in 1902), was also a prominent New York lawyer with offices on Wall Street.

Hall Park McCullough is best remembered statewide for his role as the most serious collector of Vermontiana: books, documents, ephemera, maps, diaries, manuscripts and autographs dating to the earliest days of Vermont's history. His collection was so extensive that after his death in 1966 the contents were dispersed among several institutions and some items were sold at auction. The University of Vermont obtained much of his collection and several choice items came to the Bennington Museum. A man of wealth tempered by great modesty and a strong sense of privacy, Hall Park

Richard and Editha Sterba's summer home, "Sugar Bush," originally built about 1930 by Rowland Hazard, who called it "Sugarbush." *Courtesy of Verena Sterba Michels.*

McCullough and his wife Edith Arthur "Artie" VanBenthuysen McCullough were also quietly responsible for the founding of Bennington College—she had the connections in the world of progressive higher education and he had the financial means to make things happen. After a decade of preparation, tempered by the stock market crash, Bennington College opened in the fall of 1932 as a pioneering institution for women that featured the integration of the visual and performing arts in a liberal arts curriculum, largely based on the "learn-by-doing" precepts of Vermonter John Dewey.

Far less well known is the fact that H.P. McCullough also collected parcels of land in Glastenbury, expanding on the ample base established by his grandfather. What he intended to do with these acres was anyone's guess, but he was bitten by the collector's bug and he had the wherewithal to follow his whims. According to a recollection in the 1970s of his son-in-law, William R. Scott, McCullough almost made a game of it. "He collected land in Glastenbury the way other people collect stamps," Scott once told this writer. McCullough's daughter, Ethel "Babs" Scott, liked to recall how her father used to take the family up to Glastenbury for summer picnics. She remembered having no idea why he chose a particular location, and he never mentioned that he had just purchased the site. She only learned those vital details later. In his own modest way, McCullough was exhibiting a new addition to his collection.

Indeed, Glastenbury land records in the vault of the Bennington County clerk confirm that at least thirty such transactions to Hall Park McCullough took place between 1930 and the early 1960s. A most plausible reason was that he was assembling parcels he thought should ultimately become part of the Green Mountain National Forest—which is exactly what happened a few decades later, to the public's benefit as well as to the profit of his descendants.

Hall Park McCullough (1872–1966), prominent lawyer and collector of Vermontiana, also collected parcels of Glastenbury land. *Courtesy of the Park-McCullough House.*

Well after the nineteenth-century clear-cuts had grown back, starting in the 1950s and extending into the early 1980s, a family corporation called Glastenbury Timberlands managed the McCullough and Scott properties and engaged in extensive logging. William R. Scott first managed these operations and later his sons Paul and Trenor took over. They harvested between two and two and a half million board feet of timber annually, according to Paul Scott. Details of the eventual acquisition of these lands by the Forest Service may be found in Chapter 10.

In the early days, the foresters for Glastenbury Timberlands who marked the trees and kept count of millions of board feet extracted were Maurice Winn, also a surveyor, and Edgar Killian. One worker for the Timberlands during the summer of 1955 was teacher Phillip Viereck of Shaftsbury (this writer's brother-in-law), who remembered that a sawmill was set up deep in the forest by the Cersosimo Lumber Company of Brattleboro, to which logs were skidded from a network of temporary roads and from

Dr. Richard F. Sterba (1898–1989), who studied psychoanalysis in Vienna with Sigmund Freud. *Courtesy of Verena Sterba Michels.*

Dr. Editha Sterba (1894–1986), also studied with Freud and held a doctorate in musicology. *Courtesy of Verena Sterba Michels.*

which dimension lumber was trucked out to the firm's headquarters. Other contractors were engaged at various times.

Viereck recalled that one of his duties was to follow around the foresters and take notes. Another task was to eliminate certain trees of low market value, mainly soft maples, by making four hatchet cuts through the bark and applying an herbicide. That technique was later rejected on the theory that it could be harmful to wildlife. "There were logging roads everywhere, with one main road into it," he said. A main road went in the east, or Somerset, side of town, through a gate that was locked on nights and weekends, Viereck remembered.

Winn recalled that the principal road into the tract of some five thousand acres followed an old logging railroad that was originally built to facilitate construction of the hydroelectric Somerset dam in 1912. Killian and Winn managed a wood manufacturing operation in Woodford Hollow, the Draper Corporation, whose parent company, located in Hopedale, Massachusetts, made looms and other textile machinery. The remains of Draper's Woodford building can still be seen amid a mobile home settlement along the Molly Stark Trail. That mill churned out millions of textile bobbins from maples that grew in northern Woodford and southern Glastenbury. Its demise was related to the general migration of textiles from New England to the South.

Among parcels McCullough did not acquire were approximately 350 acres held by Rowland Hazard, whose name, along with that of his daughter Caroline, appears on the final 1936 list of Glastenbury town officers.

Here is where the story of Glastenbury intersects, amazingly, with two international giants of twentieth-century psychiatry: Carl Jung and Sigmund Freud. As noted in the previous chapter, Rowland Hazard was a highly successful American businessman. A graduate of Yale in 1903, he had served from 1914 to 1916 as a state senator in his home state of Rhode Island, where he was born in 1881. A Republican, he was a delegate to the 1912 national party convention that renominated President William Howard Taft. Hazard served in World War I and was first associated with his family's woolen textile business, the Peace Dale Manufacturing Company, which had prospered making blankets for the army in the Civil War. He later established a ranch in southern New Mexico, where he started La Luz Clay Products Co., which tapped a vein of quality clay to make floor and roofing tiles. Hazard was also involved in manufacturing in Waterbury, Connecticut; was a director of Allied Chemical & Dye Co., the Rhode Island Hospital Trust and the Interlaken Iron Co.; and held a partnership in a New York brokerage house.

Yet despite all his business successes, Hazard was plagued by addiction to alcohol. In a vain effort to stop drinking he consulted with Carl Jung—the founder of the school of analytical psychology, who had split with Freud. Jung told Hazard that only a spiritual conversion of some sort would enable him to be free from the powerful compulsion to drink. Hazard became associated with the Oxford Group, a Christian organization that sought divine guidance for conditions such as alcoholism, and he was helpful in inspiring Bill Wilson ("Bill W.") of East Dorset and "Dr. Bob" Smith, originally from St. Johnsbury, to form Alcoholics Anonymous, though Hazard never joined AA himself.

For several months in 1933 and 1934 Hazard was so incapacitated by alcoholism that he was hospitalized. Yet he was able during August 1934 to help rescue another alcoholic, Edwin "Ebby" Thacher, from being sentenced to the Brattleboro Retreat, then known as Vermont's insane asylum. Hazard and a friend, Cebra Graves of Bennington, persuaded Judge Collins M. Graves, Cebra's uncle, to let them take Thacher to New York where he would be placed in the care of the Oxford Group. Thacher took to the Oxford Group's philosophy with enthusiasm and brought its message in November 1934 to Bill Wilson, his old classmate from Burr and Burton Seminary in Manchester, Vermont—a development that led to the formation of Alcoholics Anonymous and its twelve-step program for recovery. The episode has become a memorable, even venerable, event in AA history and has earned Hazard the reputation of having been "the messenger of the messenger" in the creation of AA.

Throughout World War II, Hazard had recovered to the extent that he served as vice-president and general manager of the Bristol Manufacturing Company of Waterbury, Connecticut, and in fact died of a coronary occlusion while at work in that company's office on December 20, 1945, at the age of sixty-four. His final days were difficult indeed. His eldest son, Rowland Gibson Hazard, an army captain, was killed early in World War II, and his second son, Peter, a navy pilot, went missing in action in March 1945 and was determined to have been killed in action. A third son, Charles, lived until 1961.

The Hazard property in Glastenbury, which he had acquired in 1930 and 1931 from the town itself and from Aurilla Mattison, was purchased after Hazard's death by Doctors Richard F. and Editha Sterba, who had vacationed nearby in Manchester and were looking for a secluded place to spend their summers.

The Sterbas' story is equally as fascinating as that of Rowland Hazard. Richard and Editha Sterba were both distinguished psychoanalysts who had studied with Freud and escaped from the Nazis in Vienna in 1938. Richard Sterba's diploma was signed by Freud, and both he and his wife had also studied with Freud's daughter, Anna, as well as with other prominent members of Vienna's legendary psychiatric community.

The Sterbas bought the Hazard place through a real estate agent who was reluctant to show it because of its "ghostly" legends, but these European intellectuals were too practical to accept such nonsense. They not only bought the property but also proceeded to enjoy it vigorously each summer, between Memorial Day and Labor Day, for the next forty years. They also called the place Sugarbush, but preferred to spell it "Sugar Bush."

The era of the Sterbas' residence in Glastenbury is worth describing. Few in the Bennington region knew much about them. Their years coincide with the time when Glastenbury had a population in the single low digits and for two federal censuses was officially "pop. 0." The Sterbas and their daughters Verena and Monika had a permanent home in Grosse Point, Michigan, and therefore did not get counted in Glastenbury's decennial census. During the academic year the Sterbas taught at Wayne State University and the University of Michigan.

The family's origins in Vienna are recounted in a fascinating book Dr. Richard Sterba wrote, *Reminiscences of a Viennese Psychoanalyst*, published in 1982 by Wayne State University Press. In it he relates how he emerged from a rigid, parochial, Teutonic kind of education because, thanks to his ardent interest in music and proficiency as a violinist, he was able to immerse himself in the psychiatric community and became deeply involved in the Vienna Psychoanalytical Institute. Dr. Sterba was also the author of a professional book, *Libido Theory*, published in 1942.

Though the Sterbas were not Jewish, most of their associates were, and when Hitler's Nazis took over Vienna, the Sterbas chose to emigrate to America rather than submit to a demand that they assume charge of the Freudian Society. "You didn't say no to the Nazis," said Verena, who was only two and a half years old when the family fled.

Dr. Sterba and his wife were musicians—in fact, she held doctorates in both psychology and musicology—and they combined their interests to coauthor *Beethoven and His Nephew*, published as a paperback in 1971. The book describes the way the musical genius Ludwig von Beethoven, who remained unmarried, schemed to take and maintain custody of the young son, Karl, of his deceased brother, also named Karl.

Verena Sterba, now the wife of a physician residing in Scarsdale, New York, shared with this writer some treasured memories of their many summers. It was actually Editha Sterba who initiated the purchase of the old Hazard place, Verena recalled. "My mother always talked about it as her place." They paid twenty thousand dollars for the house, including many of the Hazards' antiques and linens, with more than three hundred acres, and they thought that was far too much.

They delighted in the isolation and the wildlife, took almost daily walks to Fayville, hosted numerous summer visitors and attended to many patients who required continuity of treatment. Dr. Sterba had a cabin in the woods for his engagements with patients, who boarded in homes in Arlington or Manchester nearby. Among caretakers who watched over the place, the Sterbas hired Lloyd Mattison and after his death Herbert Ware. Another Shaftsbury resident, George Graves, would walk through the place and keep an eye on things because there was occasional vandalism. It was a seasonal house with no insulation or central heat. Dr. Sterba built a reservoir and laid in a wood pipeline to provide a gravity-fed water system, and for a time he experimented with a turbine to generate electricity.

An ever-present family activity was riding horses over the miles of old logging roads and trails. In 1953 Dr. Sterba searched for someone to help him break in a young horse, and was referred by harness maker George Small to Hendrick "Henk" Schurink, a native of Holland who was then working at Fairdale Farms in Bennington. Dr. Sterba recognized instantly that he had met a man who knew horses. And the Sterba-Schurink friendship, both professional and personal, lasted throughout the Sterbas' many summers spent at their Glastenbury home. Schurink and his wife Janet, later joined by their children, had oversight of the stables, taught equestrianship to the Sterba family and their guests and joined them on many miles of trail rides.

Henk Schurink, as a resident of Shaftsbury for more than a half century, still savors many special memories of the era of the Sterba family in Glastenbury. Every summer morning for more than thirty seasons, Schurink would drive the six miles or so up to Glastenbury from his home on Horton Hill and begin the day talking with Dr. and Mrs. Sterba over a cup of coffee. Then the equestrian nature of the day would unfold, usually with a ride on miles of old trails and logging roads. The Schurinks would ride, teach and help train the horses.

An old sugarhouse on the property was converted to a stable where four horses were kept. The Sterbas brought with them from Michigan what might be called an entourage. There was a cook, a stable hand and Mrs. Sterba's chauffeur, an African American who was always called Mr. Gibson. Besides overseeing the horses, the teaching and the riding, Schurink used to transport the horses each Memorial Day weekend from Grosse Point to Glastenbury, and then would truck them back after Labor Day.

The Sterbas had relatively little contact with the Bennington or Shaftsbury communities. In many ways their summer occupancy of a seasonal home in an unorganized Vermont town was perfect for their needs. The remoteness and solitude filled the requirement of confidentiality for the patients who came for analysis or

Memories of Glastenbury by people of a certain age include "the dog man," as he came to be known. "We used to be terrified when he came down the road," recalled Verena Sterba Michels of her summers in the 1950s.

The legend was generated by a man who chose to live alone with dozens of dogs, which became a situation that attracted rats and other problems. Many recall that the state police had to come in and shoot dogs and rats to get to the man when he was sick.

In attempting to uncover facts behind the legend, one learns that this is a story of what today would be called post-traumatic stress disorder. Knowing the facts creates a more respectful attitude. The man's name was Clyde Elwell, and he had served his nation well during World War I. He had witnessed death and destruction during his service with the 302nd Field Artillery in 1917 in France.

Elwell's way of coping with the overwhelming memories of war was to isolate himself in an ungoverned town with his Model T Ford and as many canine companions as possible. Unfortunately, the dogs were unlicensed, unvaccinated and unneutered, and their numbers grew out of control to the extent that "the dog man of Glastenbury" became a regional legend. Elwell's house was actually in Shaftsbury, adjoining the Glastenbury line, and his death record is found in the Shaftsbury vitals.

Clyde Elwell was born in Shaftsbury October 23, 1889, had worked at the Eagle Square plant, was married with two daughters and was known for playing the violin. He died in May 1958 at the age of sixty-eight at the former Veterans Administration Hospital in Northampton, Massachusetts.

treatment. The miles of wooded trails were tailor-made for their avid interest in horses. They did most of their shopping in Salem, New York, and bought meat at a favorite market in Arlington.

Schurink, as a man of much native wisdom, provided other kinds of advice on occasion. An example he recounted was when Dr. Sterba, annoyed by damage he thought might have been done by hunters, wanted to post his acreage with "no hunting" signs. But Schurink suggested that that was not a good idea because hunters, who for years had roamed those thousands of acres, might take offense in unexpected ways. The posting signs never went up. Schurink recalled meeting up with bears a few times out on the trails. Unlike anecdotes he had heard that horses are always "spooked" by bears, he said that never happened. The horses were not affected and the bears always ran away.

The Sterbas fostered an intellectual kind of community at their summer retreat and surrounded themselves with works of art as well as music. They owned some elegant paintings, and were acquainted with Rudolph Serkin and others involved in the Marlboro Music Festival. They entertained prominent guests, many from Europe. They traveled widely, lecturing around the world. Schurink remembered that Mrs. Sterba, who was "very much a lady," liked to introduce him to their guests as "Doctor Schurink" and probably enjoyed his protests about the undeserved appellation.

Through all those years, riding horses was a constant and obviously healthy activity, for Mrs. Sterba kept at it until she turned ninety. Dr. Sterba suffered a broken ankle while riding in 1978, and finally quit riding in 1986 at age eighty-eight after being knocked off his mount by a low branch.

The era of the Sterbas in Glastenbury ended with her death, in December 1986, at the age of ninety-two. Dr. Sterba suffered a stroke in 1988, and his death followed in October 1989, at age ninety-one. Both were memorialized by obituaries in the *New York Times* and other newspapers. The *Detroit Times* obituary revealed a few more details:

> *One of the highlights in the life of Dr. Richard Sterba was the day famed psychoanalyst Sigmund Freud signed his diploma in 1927. Dr. Sterba was one of the first two graduates of the Vienna Psychoanalytic Institute in Austria.*
>
> *Dr. Sterba, who fled Nazi rule in Europe to bring his family to the United States, also was an accomplished violinist, an author, an art collector. . . A graduate of the University of Vienna Medical School before entering the Vienna Institute, Dr. Sterba rejected an offer to be director of the institute—because he felt he would have been under Nazi rule after Austria was annexed by Hitler's Germany in 1938.*
>
> *Strongly opposed to Nazi doctrines, Dr. Sterba, of Czechoslovakian-Austrian heritage, refused to present a paper in 1936 at the Nazi-dominated Berlin Institute of Psychotherapy unless one of his Jewish colleagues were invited first. In 1938, Dr. Sterba, still refusing to buckle under Nazi pressure, persuaded the father of a patient he was treating to deposit the fees in a Swiss bank account. With that money, he and his family came to Detroit after considerable difficulty.*
>
> *Their story was the basis of a 1943 fictionalized account by Laura Z. Hobson, "The Trespassers."*

Another vital element of their escape was provided by Henry Schurink. Dr. Sterba persuaded the Nazis in 1938 that he had a very important patient in Holland who needed treatment, and he was allowed to travel there, with his family. They never returned to Vienna.

Chapter 10

GLASTENBURY, RECREATIONAL MECCA, IN THE NEWS

In September 1979 a newspaper story—splashed across the top of the *Bennington Banner*'s front page—reported that an agreement had been reached for the first ever purchase of lands in Glastenbury by the U.S. Forest Service. It was big news in southwestern Vermont because, while towns like Sunderland and Woodford already had the major portion of their territory in federal hands, Glastenbury had been a conspicuous omission on maps of the Green Mountain National Forest since its inception in 1932. The sellers were the grown children of William R. Scott and his wife, Ethel "Babs" McCullough Scott, the daughter of the parcel collector, Hall Park McCullough.

The announcement, while accurate, was somewhat premature because of politics and bureaucracy. The political element was that September 1979 was near the end of the Jimmy Carter's presidency, when it was assumed that federal funds were available for a purchase of this size. After Ronald Reagan was elected, this kind of money had nearly dried up. Bureaucracy was involved because the transfer of land to the Forest Service is a time-consuming affair, wrapped in miles of red tape and reams of paperwork. "It was a tortuous process," recalled Paul Scott, one of the descendants who, doing business as the Glastenbury Corporation, sold the large parcels along with his brother Trenor and their sister Virginia Scott Sterling.

The net result was that some 96 percent of the entire town of Glastenbury was sold to the National Forest in four major segments over a period of seventeen years between 1981 and 1998. The transactions were so large and the transfer so significant that it seems worth taking the space in a town history to spell out details.

The first and largest transaction, a total of ninety-seven hundred acres in two parcels that included Lost Pond, as well as vast acreage to the west and north of the mountain summit, was sold for $1,843,000 on February 13, 1981. It included a two-hundred-foot easement or buffer around the Appalachian–Long Trail as well as certain specified timber-cutting rights to the Glastenbury Corporation for ten years.

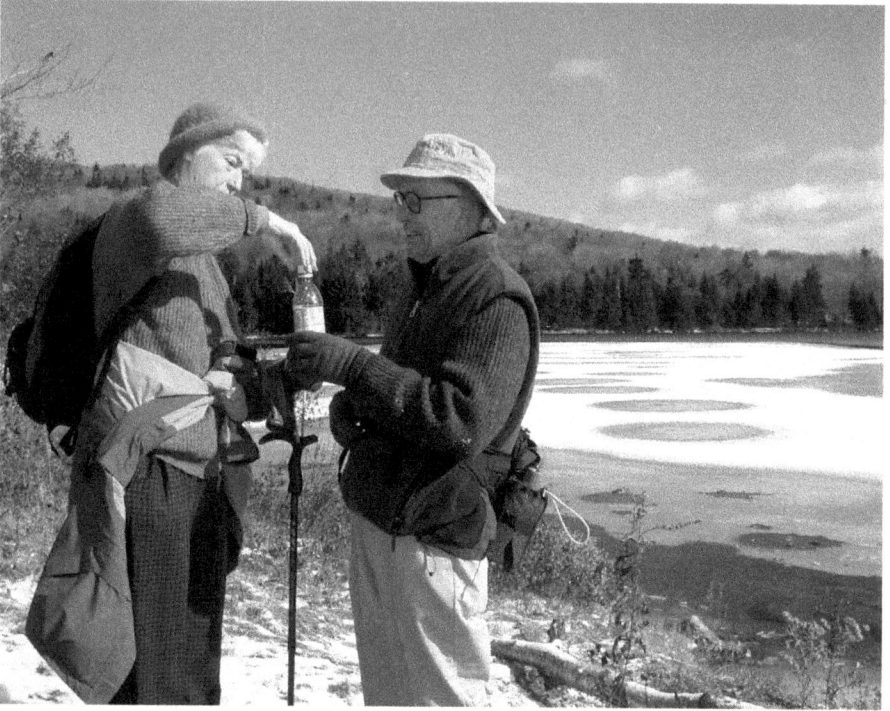

Charles Yoder, who chaired the Glastenbury Zoning Board and was also a selectman in Shaftsbury, is shown on an outing at frozen Little Pond in November 2002, with Ruth Rehfus. Charles died in 2006. *Courtesy of Dick Andrews, Forest Watch.*

The second parcel of around seventy-one hundred acres along the Somerset border—touching both Sunderland on the north and Woodford on the south—transferred on December 27, 1985, for $1,420,000. Two ten-acre holdings were exempted for the owners of private camps.

The third transaction followed on April 16, 1986, with a parcel of fifty-eight hundred acres—a huge chunk of virtually the entire southwest corner of the town—for $1,305,000. Again the holders of two other ten-acre private camp parcels were exempted. Sellers were identified in the deeds of these three transactions as the siblings Paul and Trenor Scott and Virginia Scott Sterling and their spouses along with attorney John H. Williams and his wife Deborah.

Finally, not until December 17, 1998, did the last 4,030 acres transfer, for $1,775,000. This included two non-contiguous parcels in the northwest and southeast parts of the town, the latter a mostly marshy territory known as Castle Meadow. This transaction was handled through an intermediary, the Trust for Public Lands.

The grand total of these sales was 26,630 acres for $6,343,000. The chain of title to thousands of forested acres that had started with Trenor W. Park becoming involved in a nineteenth-century logging railroad, then continued with his grandson, Hall Park

Above: Meg Cottam, one of today's six residents of Glastenbury, is photographed inside the fire tower at the top of the mountain, the sixth highest in Vermont, along with Terry Eubanks, formerly of Bennington. *Courtesy of Dick Andrews, Forest Watch.*

Left: Mollie Matteson, associate director of Forest Watch, on cross-country skis, poses near Little Pond before a large beech tree that had been scratched by a climbing black bear. *Courtesy of Dick Andrews, Forest Watch.*

The old Goddard shelter, about a half mile south of the summit of Glastenbury, hosted many years of hikers on the Appalachian and Long Trails. The photo was taken in August 2002. The shelter has been demolished and replaced with a better one by the Green Mountain Club. *Courtesy of Dick Andrews, Forest Watch.*

McCullough, the persistent parcel collector, had almost come to an end. If acquisition by the U.S. Forest Service had been McCullough's goal, then a large long-term wish had been achieved.

Of the remaining privately owned land, McCullough's grandson, Trenor Scott, still owns some eleven hundred acres around Fayville. The rest is divided among the Robert G. Scott estate, Rickey L. Harrington and Thomas Gallagher, as will be described in Chapter 12 with a description of the town's grand list.

Glastenbury was also in the news frequently during the 1970s when the location of the Long Trail was changed—twice. For nonhikers it needs to be explained that the famed Appalachian Trail that links Springer Mountain, Georgia, and Mount Katahdin, Maine, coexists with part of Vermont's 251-mile Long Trail that links Massachusetts and Canada. The two trails split near Killington Mountain as the AT heads east toward New Hampshire and the LT continues north toward Canada.

Glastenbury Camp, one of the earliest overnight huts for hikers on Vermont's Long Trail. *Courtesy of Mark Haugwout.*

The original AT-LT from Route 9, Vermont's Molly Stark Trail, to the summit of Glastenbury was not only boring and lacked scenic vistas, but much of it followed old roads that were subject to eroding "freshets," and the experience did not fulfill the Long Trail's philosophy of "a footpath in the wilderness." The trail was shifted temporarily to the west via Bald Mountain, the highest point in the town of Bennington (2,857 feet), and followed a trail called the West Ridge to the summit. Finally, in 1977 the official trail was moved to the east, where a large trailhead parking area was built. A 90-foot suspension bridge spans a brook with the ironic name of City Stream and the trail offers scenic lookouts and a more compatible ambience, though somewhat longer than the original Long Trail route.

Glastenbury also made the news in 1977 when some enterprising editor remembered the fortieth anniversary of the disincorporation of Glastenbury and Somerset. The occasion was marked by newspaper articles and notably by a history oriented editorial in the *Bennington Banner* on the precise anniversary, December 31, 1977:

GLASTENBURY

Along the old Long Trail near the summit of Glastenbury. There was no view until you reached the summit, and even then you had to climb the fire tower for a panoramic vista of the vast expanse of undulating Green Mountains.

Forty years ago tonight two Vermont towns disappeared. Glastenbury and Somerset held equal voting power with Burlington or Rutland in the Vermont House, but on the twelfth stroke of midnight, Dec. 31, 1937, they were stripped of legal standing as municipalities. Their populations were almost gone, and these towns that once supported hundreds of loggers and dozens of hardscrabble farms reverted to the deer and bobcat...

Benning Wentworth, governor of New Hampshire, chartered both towns in 1761 and settlers moved in shortly afterwards. In the northwest corner of Glastenbury a small settlement grew up along Peter's Branch. By 1810, Glastenbury's population had risen to 76, but soon after began the first of many migrations away. The winter seemed to last all year in 1816 (eighteen hundred-and-froze-to-death, as it is remembered). Through Vermont, people left the rocky, niggardly soil behind and headed for western New York and the prairie lands opening beyond...

The wood of Glastenbury like the oil wells that fuel our economy today, was limited. By 1889, Glastenbury had been shaved of its precious crop and only stubble remained. The railroad stopped in 1889, and in 1890 came the first of several mortgage foreclosures.

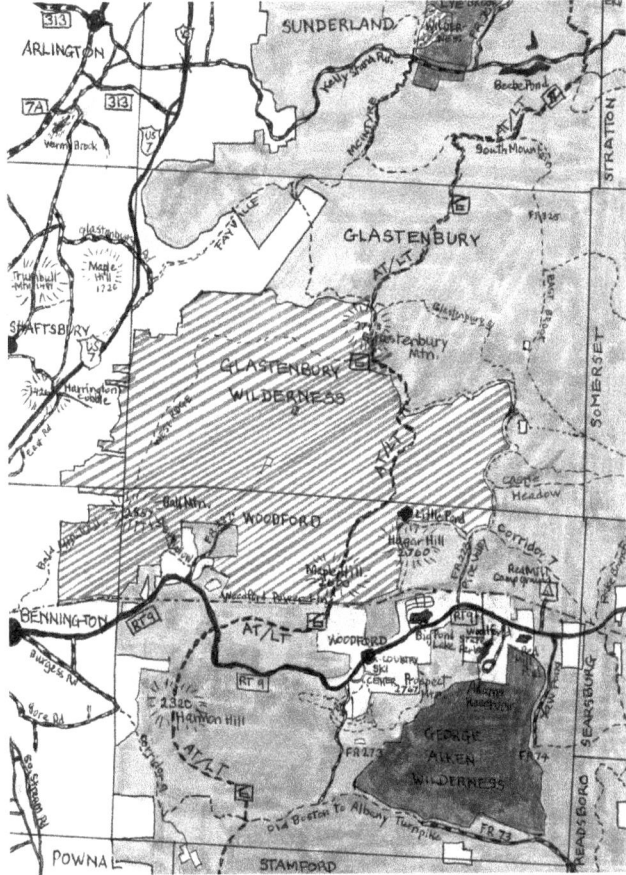

Map shows boundaries of the Glastenbury Wilderness district, adopted by Congress in 2006, which covers most of the southern half of Glastenbury including the summit. Wilderness extends well into the north end of Woodford, and reaches into parts of Bennington and Shaftsbury. *Sketch by Ellen K. Viereck, based on Green Mountain National Forest's website map.*

In more recent years the issue of Wilderness (with a capital W), as noted, was debated in fairly heated language at times, climaxing with the 2006 act of Congress that placed forty-two thousand acres of Vermont woodland in perpetually protected status. A sample of the resulting publicity might be seen in the May 2007 edition of *AMC Outdoors*, the magazine of the Appalachian Mountain Club, which featured on its cover an article headlined "Go Wild: The path to New England's newest Wilderness areas." It reported on the 2006 New England Wilderness Act that added some seventy thousand acres to permanently protected status. The act created three new Wilderness areas and expanded four others on National Forest land in New Hampshire and Vermont. Ed Winchester, the executive editor and publisher, wrote:

> *Visitors to New Hampshire's new Wild River Wilderness, and the Battell and Glastenbury Mountain Wilderness areas in Vermont will never again hear an engine's drone or the revving of a chain saw. In time, wildlife biologists will no longer lament the loss of Eastern old growth. Recovering second-growth forest will have, in effect, recovered.*

The Glastenbury fire tower in the 1940s. *Courtesy of Mark Haugwout.*

Another article explained the history of Wilderness in New England, tracing it to the Wilderness Act of 1964, which had been promoted by the late Senator George D. Aiken of Vermont and was signed into law by President Lyndon B. Johnson. Two more rounds of Wilderness designations followed in 1975 and 1984, which set aside more than 260,000 acres in New England. The most recent legislation was originally set to add 48,000 acres in Vermont, but politics reared its head in response to pressure from snowmobile and timber interests, and that number was reduced to 42,000, most of the cuts taken at the expense of Glastenbury territory. There had been much hope that the Glastenbury Wilderness could expand to join up with the existing Lye Brook Wilderness in Sunderland, the town just to the north. Perhaps that goal can someday be achieved.

The thrust of the Appalachian Mountain Club's "What is Wilderness" article was to state the case for the economic benefits of Wilderness. It quoted real estate spokesmen

Chet Mallory of Bennington (1919–1998) was the full-time resident of the Glastenbury fire tower during World War II. *Courtesy of Dorothy Mallory*.

O ccasionally Glastenbury appears in the news in an unexpected place. Before I was married I lived for a time in an apartment in the North Bennington home of an energetic elderly woman named Marjorie Eddy Nash Ludlow. She loved to talk about her experiences of hiking in the Adirondacks and Green Mountains, usually with her late brother, C. Howard Nash. I don't remember her mentioning Glastenbury. But a mutual friend who heard that I was writing about Glastenbury suggested that I check out Mr. Nash's obituary. Sure enough, after he died at age 83 in December 1960, it mentioned that at the age of 58 he had become enthusiastic about hiking to mountaintops. He had hiked to all 48 peaks of 4,000 feet in New York State, many with his sister, Mrs. Ludlow. He had traversed the entire Long Trail from Blackinton, Massachusetts (a neighborhood in North Adams), to North Troy, Vermont, on the Canadian border. And he had hiked to the top of Glastenbury Mountain 153 times! Surely that's a record that no one will ever surpass.

and others in the business community who recognize the value of nearby territory that enhances the quality of life, offers protection for wildlife habitat and attracts tourism.

One of Vermont's premier environmental organizations is Green Mountain Forest Watch, headquartered in Richmond. Because this writer is a former member of the board of Forest Watch, and because our thoughts coincide quite precisely, a statement about the recreational significance of Glastenbury was solicited from that organization.

> *Glastenbury is a recreational resource almost unique in the Northeast. Mostly public land and nearly uninhabited, it is the largest unsettled and unroaded tract in Vermont, and is a major part of one of very few large areas of land that show up as inky black regions in satellite photos taken at night. Just thinking about exploring Glastenbury lifts the spirits of those who share the lament of ecologist Aldo Leopold in his 1949 environmental classic, A Sand County Almanac:*
>
> > *"Man always kills the thing he loves, and so we the pioneers have killed our wilderness. Some say we had to. Be that as it may, I am glad I shall never be young without wild country to be young in. Of what avail are forty freedoms without a blank spot on the map?"*
>
> *Pioneers were, of course, very active in Glastenbury, but it continues to steadily recover its wildness. While not literally a blank spot on the map, it is as close as one is likely to get in the lower 48 states. In December 2006, Congress designated the 22,400-acre central portion bounded by snowmobile trails as Wilderness, where natural processes will continue undisturbed and motorized use is excluded.*

Conservationists, particularly Forest Watch, had urged designation of a 40,000-acre Glastenbury Wilderness extending all the way north to Kelley Stand Road. Combined with an expanded Lye Brook Wilderness, this would have anchored one of the largest protected wild areas in the Northeast. Such a designation would have allowed hiking, hunting, fishing and other non-motorized use to continue, while prohibiting logging and motor vehicles. With machinery barred from the summit of Glastenbury Mountain, the Wilderness would have ensured an unrivaled resource of year-round remoteness and tranquility for all time. If political will develops, it is still a possibility for the future.

Even diminished as it is, Glastenbury Wilderness is big—almost the size of an entire Vermont township. It attracts hikers, backpackers, snowshoers, cross-country skiers and hunters lured by extensive backcountry. The Green Mountain Club, which maintains the Long Trail and Appalachian Trail through Glastenbury, describes the view from the historic fire tower on the summit of Glastenbury Mountain (3,748 feet) as "more wilderness than is to be seen from any other point on the Long Trail." To reach the tower by the Long Trail requires 10 miles of walking from either the south or the north. There are shorter ways, but the shortest is still 14 miles for a hiker with an ordinary car who chooses not to bushwhack.

As well as challenging, Glastenbury is beautiful and varied, from Little Pond (a two-mile hike north from Route 9 on Forest Road 275) to the old beaver ponds in the headwaters of the Black Brook ravine to the thick spruce and fir forest on the summit dome of the mountain itself. Bears, moose and reclusive species of birds find refuge in Glastenbury's vastness.

Despite Glastenbury's size, five shelters on the twenty-mile stretch of the Long Trail between Vermont Route 9 and the Kelley Stand Road enable leisurely exploration on and near the trail; three of these shelters are in the township of Glastenbury itself. Detailed information is in the Green Mountain Club's Long Trail Guide ($14.95, www. greenmountainclub.org). The guide also describes the moderate day hikes to the summit of Bald Mountain in the southwestern corner of the Wilderness, and the long, remote West Ridge Trail, which can be combined with the Long Trail for more ambitious trail-based hiking. Parking options are also indicated.

For more adventurous exploration away from marked trails, one can consult topographic maps available at Green Mountain National Forest offices for six dollars each. Woodford, Sunderland and Bennington quadrangles are most useful. Former forest roads, some of which are now de facto handicap-accessible wilderness routes, are clearly shown. Streams and ridges provide enticing but challenging or even risky routes. Many ancient logging trails and other routes shown on the maps are fast fading, or have completely disappeared long ago. Use your compass, the map and your head. Glastenbury is big enough to get lost in.

Glastenbury's lofty summit has often been considered as a site for wind power and was actually involved in Vermont's very first experiment in wind generation before World War II. An early book on the subject, *Power from the Wind*, by Palmer Cosslett Putnam, published in 1948, describes a research station in which a gas-heated anemometer was

Chet Mallory in front of his year-round cabin atop Glastenbury Mountain in the 1940s. *Courtesy of Dorothy Mallory.*

A wood-burning cookstove from the 1920s was a feature of Chet Mallory's mountaintop cabin. *Courtesy of Dorothy Mallory.*

mounted atop Glastenbury 80 feet above the ground and 40 feet above the trees. It operated for 212 days, from March 2 to September 30, 1941. But in the end, the decision was that Glastenbury was simply too remote—too far from roads and power lines—and the extreme elevation would risk damage from ice. So a decision was made to locate a 125-megawatt turbine on a mere 2,000-foot mountain, Grandpa's Knob, near Rutland, that met the criteria.

The lines of Central Vermont Public Service Corporation, Vermont's largest electric utility, were fed by winds on Grandpa's Knob starting on October 19, 1941, until one of the eight-ton blades snapped on March 26, 1945. The device was never repaired because of wartime priorities and constraints, so although the wind-generating experiment was a success, Vermonters knew little about it because of the dominance of war news and because the broken blade was never repaired.

In more recent times Glastenbury has been considered for further wind-generating sites but the distance from existing power lines and roads was always the deciding factor. At the time of this writing, the only wind turbines in Vermont were located about forty miles southeast of Glastenbury in the town of Searsburg, where eleven towers placed by the Green Mountain Power Corporation fed six megawatts into the New England grid.

An important structure in Glastenbury is the steel fire lookout tower at the summit, which in recent times has been restored so it is safe to climb. From the enclosed lookout on a clear day a most magnificent panorama of Vermont territory can be slowly and visually inhaled. The tower itself was built by the Vermont Timberland Owners Association in 1927–28 following a century of unregulated logging practices and a series of droughts that had elevated the danger of forest fires. The year 1927 carried an environmental wake-up call to Vermonters when a record-setting November flood caused many fatalities and massive damage to highways and bridges, underscoring the need for flood as well as fire control.

At one time there were thirty-eight fire towers on mountaintops in Vermont, but Glastenbury's is now one of only twelve still standing. Its use as a tower with which to spot fires actually ended in 1947–48, and it fell into disrepair as aerial surveillance was utilized to discover smoke in the forests. The tower was rehabilitated and made safe to climb in 2005 by the Green Mountain Club and the Forest Service.

During World War II a year-round lookout was hired, both to spot fires and also possible enemy planes, plus conduct duties that involved weather and wind velocity readings. The job was handled by Chet Mallory of Bennington, who had been a summer lookout there since 1937. Then for two winters during the war he braved powerful winds and frigid temperatures living in a mountaintop cabin that featured an old-fashioned wood-burning kitchen stove. Mallory once told an interviewer that he had no trouble with porcupines until someone climbed the tower's wooden steps with bare feet. He also recalled trying to keep warm at night by heating stones to warm his bed.

Chapter 11

NEW ZONING LAW FOILS
UNWISE DEVELOPMENT

After Dr. Editha Sterba died in 1986, her husband placed the 340-acre property on the real estate market. In 1987 an option to acquire it was purchased by a firm—Properties of America Inc., then headquartered nearby in Williamstown, Massachusetts—that specialized in the acquisition and resale of large parcels. The $10,000 option was toward a reported purchase price of $400,000.

Properties of America was proposing to sell house lots at two thousand to twenty-five hundred dollars an acre, and the idea was that each lot owner would request a conditional permit from a rudimentary zoning ordinance to build a house. The land was divided into sixteen potential building lots, an average of twenty-one and a quarter acres each, for single-family houses. If all went well, the developers stood to double their investment.

But Glastenbury has a strong, silent constituency of admirers, and the scheme soon attracted formidable opposition. With help from the Bennington County Regional Commission (BCRC), an interim zoning ordinance was quickly adopted that divided Glastenbury's private land—that is, not owned by the National Forest—into two districts. Forest One zone, in the lowest elevation westerly portion of town, covered most of the former Hazard-Sterba property, and would allow permanent dwellings, as a conditional use only, and on a twenty-five-acre minimum lot. Every zoning change, in fact, was made a conditional use, subject to review by a zoning board of adjustment first appointed by the BCRC and confirmed by the supervisor. Forest Two zone, the remainder of the town, provided only for seasonal camps and would not even allow septic tanks. The vast majority of the town held by the National Forest is exempt from local zoning provisions.

The new law was adopted in December 1987 after a public hearing by the town's legislative body, which at that time consisted of Supervisor Barbara MacIntyre of Bennington and no one else. If it appears unseemly in Vermont, which has such a tradition of town government close to the people and where everything is done by majority vote, for a lone public official to "adopt" an ordinance, that is the way the office of supervisor of unorganized towns and gores works. The supervisor in an unorganized town, appointed by the governor, is "close to the people" because there are so few people.

So the new zoning would not support Properties of America's plan for sixteen permanent habitations. At best, seven twenty-five-acre lots might fit into the Forest One zone. The subdividers petitioned for a zoning change to expand Forest One to fit nine house lots into the sector where permanent housing was conditionally allowed. Thus prompted, Supervisor MacIntyre published notices of a public hearing to be held March 3, 1988, at the Bennington County Courthouse in Bennington, to consider the Glastenbury zoning applications for conditional use. The notice included two maps, one showing the current zoning and another of a proposed change in districts.

According to the account in the *Bennington Banner*, fifty-six people attended the hearing, an astonishing expression of concern in a town that could boast (at that time) only two inhabitants. It turned out that all of those attending, except for two agents from Properties of America Inc., opposed the zoning change. One of the agents, Gregory Harrison, won no friends when he refused, under persistent questioning, to name the civil engineer he said had made satisfactory percolation tests of the soil, tests that would permit septic tanks and leach fields.

Harrison and his sidekick found themselves surrounded. Because of the lack of municipal services, and because the only road access enters from East Road in Shaftsbury, any new residence in Glastenbury would depend on services available in Shaftsbury, meaning primarily the volunteer fire department and the public elementary school. At the hearing, Shaftsbury fire officials said they would not assume such added responsibilities. The fire department said, in effect, that coverage of its own thirty-six square miles of populated township was already spread thin. A similar story was told by the Shaftsbury School Board, which would not commit itself to accept extra tuition pupils, even at the going rate of thirty-two hundred dollars a year.

While the Shaftsbury Elementary School had a capacity of 410 students and only 356 were then enrolled, explained board Chairman Andrew Bacchi, the principal was committed to small classes. Because of these strictures, no third- or fourth-grade pupils could be accepted on a tuition basis. Another major concern was the nonavailability of fire insurance. It followed that if no fire department took responsibility for the territory, insurance coverage was unlikely and therefore mortgages could not be obtained.

Chairman Gedeon LaCroix of the BCRC told the hearing that his executive committee had rejected placing all the Sterba land in the Forest One zone. If they had, the Properties of America proposition would have been facilitated. Though a public hearing had been warned on the matter, he said, no one from Properties of America had appeared to challenge that decision. Others expressed concern about possible loss of uninhabited lands for hunting, hiking, horseback riding, cross-country skiing, snowmobiling and other recreational uses.

To test the strength of opposition to the zoning change, MacIntyre consulted with attorney Robert E. Woolmington, whom she had engaged as counsel for the town, and then called for an advisory standing vote. Not a person stood to support the developers' plans. Shortly afterward, Properties of America Inc. withdrew its proposal and forfeited the option. Soon after that, the firm declared bankruptcy.

The impromptu zoning ordinance had indeed served its purpose, and the regional commission had played a vital role in helping to tame an ungoverned territory that meant a great deal to residents of Bennington County.

But many still wondered what marketplace whim would determine the future of Glastenbury.

Chapter 12

A TWENTY-FIRST-CENTURY TOUR OF THE OLD GHOST TOWN

Here is a brief rundown of today's old "ghost town" of Glastenbury, an unorganized municipality of very few residents but the subject of a great deal of public interest in a wide radius throughout Vermont and elsewhere. Former Governor Hiland Hall's description from the 1860s still fits: "One of the roughest and most mountainous towns in the state . . . a pretty safe place of retreat for bears and other wild animals."

One way to think of it, and perhaps to focus some new perspective on the matter, is that Glastenbury is a town of some twenty-seven thousand acres (in round numbers), twenty-six thousand of which now belong to the Green Mountain National Forest. At this writing those thousand or so privately owned acres contain a total of two full-time households and two seasonal homes—one of them modest and the other grand—for a total of six inhabitants on record. (In some places one sees a year 2000 census figure of sixteen, which is erroneous and must have been totaled by an enumerator who went into Glastenbury, turned right at the principal T intersection, crossed back into Shaftsbury and began counting residents in the wrong town.) Scattered through the twenty-six thousand acres are four camps on private parcels of about ten acres each.

The old village of Fayville today is a relatively level clearing of perhaps fifty acres. There are no buildings standing but a rummaging around will discover a few cellar holes, though most of those are gradually closing up, as Robert Frost put it, "like a dent in dough." It is a pleasant hike into Fayville, about a mile and a half from where you can park a car, around the T intersection at the end of the Glastenbury Road near the Robert Scott estate.

The old village of South Glastenbury, once the terminus of a railroad, is also devoid of any buildings and reachable by a modest hike. Here, one begins at the Harbour Road off Route 9 in Woodford and a car can be driven until prevented from traveling farther by a bridge that has a locked gate. From this point it is a hike of perhaps a mile and a half along the old railroad right of way to the former settlement at "the forks" of Bolles Brook. This is also the route of the old Long Trail, and it passes an attractive new red-roofed log camp owned by the Lauzon family. The east fork of the brook is crossed by a bridge, just beyond

The Robert G. Scott estate, an expansive seasonal residence, was built in 1989 on the site of the former Hazard and Sterba summer homes.

which is the site of the loggers' boardinghouse that was converted into a summer resort hotel, though no sign of it is evident today. On a steep hillside to the east one can find the cellar hole of the decorative Casino building. Jumbles of brick and iron bands mark locations of charcoal kilns but much of that evidence has been covered by years of forest duff.

A tour of the town's public records might begin with a grand list, which in most towns fills hundreds of pages. In Glastenbury it takes two pages and shows nine landowners of record in addition to the largest, the U.S. Forest Service. The grand list totals $21,589, which is 1 percent of its presumed fair market value, placing that total at $2,158,900. (To that figure the state applies a formula called the common level of appraisal, or CLA, which in this case is 79.4 percent, meaning it is that degree below real fair market value, suggesting that a reappraisal is due.) All of these owners except for Supervisor Harrington pay a higher nonresident statewide tax rate. The total tax imposed on these properties in 2006 was $48,625.02, less a 5 percent stipend to the supervisor (his fee) of $2,431.25. Glastenbury's total tax rates for 2006 were set at $0.95 for the base homestead rate and $1.44 for nonresidential.

The National Forest pays what is called a "pilot" fee, or "payment in lieu of taxes," based on acreage the federal government holds. In 2006 this totaled $26,240, or close to $1 per acre of ownership.

Maple Hill Cemetery on the East Road in Shaftsbury, not far from the Glastenbury Road, is where most burials of Glastenbury residents took place. It is a town that never had a church or a cemetery of its own.

Tax revenue from an unorganized town goes to the state, and one benefit is that the state agency of transportation maintains and plows the roads, whereas other towns take care of their own local roads.

The largest Glastenbury taxpayer is Robert G. Scott, whose total bill for 2006 was $32,746.10 for both his large seasonal home and that of the caretaker's family, and 338 acres of land. The tax bill is sent to his home in Manhattan.

It was this Scott family, no relation to Trenor Scott the descendant of Trenor Park, who in 1988 answered the question of what would be the future of Glastenbury by purchasing the Sterba property, once targeted as a housing development. The old wooden Hazard-Sterba house that had hosted several decades of sophisticated summer visitors was torched while the Shaftsbury Fire Department was paid to stand by so fire didn't spread to the forest. On its site was built a massive homestead of timber and stone, to be used for "occasional seasonal use but not permanent occupancy" by order of the then new Glastenbury zoning board on May 30, 1989. The board was composed of Charles E. Dewey III of Bennington as chairman, Suzanne dePeyster of Sandgate, Ferdinand Bongartz of Manchester and Charles Yoder of Shaftsbury. The board stipulated that if there was any future impact on the tax structure, a variance would have to be sought. The Scott house, based on data in the three zoning permits it has received

Rickey L. Harrington, the Glastenbury supervisor, in the office of his log home in the newest house in town.

since 1989, totals more than fifteen thousand square feet of living space. On the site of the Sterbas' former riding ring, a separate handsome timber-frame, two-story house was built for the family of the full-time caretaker.

Robert G. Scott has kept a low profile in the Bennington County community but is known in the world of business and finance as a top executive of Morgan Stanley, the global financial services firm. When visitors to Glastenbury get too close to the Scott estate they are likely to encounter Dennis Madden, the caretaker, who may inquire as to their intentions.

Both Dennis Madden and his wife, Meg Cottam, have served as the town's representatives on the Bennington Regional Planning Commission, which takes special oversight interest in Glastenbury. Another prominent part-time resident is Thomas Gallagher, the former superintendent of the Southwest Vermont Supervisory Union, the region's public school system. Mr. and Mrs. Gallagher resided in the old Ira Mattison homestead while he was superintendent, modernized it and ran a llama farm. They have retained ownership now that he has moved on to Rome, New York.

Newest residents are Rickey and Donna Harrington, who moved in April 2000 to an attractive log home they built well off any beaten path. Harrington gave up his seat on the Shaftsbury School Board to move to Glastenbury, and a conditional-use permit for construction of the house was granted by the zoning board.

TOWN OF GLASTENBURY

Glastenbury, Vermont

PROPERTY TAX BILL – TAX YEAR 2005

For period beginning April 1, 2005 and ending March 31, 2006

Property Owner: Central Vermont Public Service Corp.
                  77 Grove Street
                  Rutland , Vermont 05701

SPAN # 240-258-10001   Property Description :
.   Utility Lines , etc.

Parcel Size (acres) : --------------
Total *ACCESSED* *VALUE* *$*_____

    Municipal Rate :   0.50   Tax : $101.00
    Statewide Education Rate :   1.81   Tax : $364.80
    .Total Tax Rate :   2.31   Total Tax : $465.80   *Pd. in Full*
                                                         8/15/06

Homestead Value :

N/A

Tax in the amount of $465.80 is due and payable on or before
August 15 , 2006. Remit check to :

    Rickey L. Harrington , Supervisor
    Town of Glastenbury
    1185 Glastenbury Road
    Shaftsbury , Vermont 05262

An eight percent penalty will be charged on any amount unpaid
on the due date, plus maximum interest as provided by law.

Home of Bigfoot

A sample tax bill from the town of Glastenbury-this one for the electric utility, Central Vermont Public Service Corp.-features "Big Foot," a humorous invention of Supervisor Rickey L. Harrington.

Owners of record of Glastenbury camps, with about 10 acres each, are Larry and Eugene Lauzon of Bennington; Christine Cross and others of Eagle Bridge, New York; Robert Lincoln of Clarksburg, Massachusetts; and David and Lisa Sausville of Addison. Trenor Scott, who lives in Oregon, the descendant of the Hall, Park and McCullough families, owns 1,153 acres out of the thousands his ancestors once held. A tax bill is also sent to Central Vermont Public Service Corporation, the electric utility, which owns lines in the town. That covers everyone on the grand list.

The current supervisor of unorganized towns and gores for Bennington County, Rickey Harrington, who calculates and sends the tax bills, works out of his home in a metal design and fabrication business. There is a board of listers, or appraisers: Barbara Andrejczak of Manchester and Jeanne Zoppel of Sandgate. An official list of all citizens who have served as supervisor in the past has eluded this author's search, but those names, besides Barbara MacIntyre, would include William Myers of Shaftsbury, Ferdinand Bongartz of Manchester, Larry Malloy of Arlington, Paul Bohne III and Mary N. Geannelis of Bennington, Edie Jordan of Sunderland and William J. Fisk of Shaftsbury.

James Henderson, a BCRC staff member, who has demonstrated close interest in Glastenbury ever since he began working on the town plan and zoning ordinance in the late 1980s, is the town's part-time administrator, taking care chiefly of zoning applications and enforcement. Henderson's slide show of Glastenbury, featuring color aerial vistas as well as historic photographs, has proved popular on several occasions. He has also worked to revise the zoning ordinance and smooth out some "boilerplate" provisions that were hastily enacted in the original version. Zoning board members at the time of this writing were Barbara MacIntyre of Bennington, Ellen K. Viereck, Cinda Morse and this writer, all of Shaftsbury, and one vacancy to be filled by the supervisor.

The town has been represented in the state legislature for the past decade by Representative Alice Miller, a Democrat, whose district covers the towns of Shaftsbury and Glastenbury plus a few houses in eastern Bennington to make up an equitable number of voters relative to other districts. The forest fire warden is David McKeighan, a former Shaftsbury fire chief, who once worked as a caretaker for the Sterbas.

Why is all this important? In this first decade of the twenty-first century, when so much of the landscape of these United States has been malled, paved, urbanized, suburbanized or otherwise sprawled, and limitless "economic growth" is a driving force of the economy, interest in a place like Glastenbury remains powerful because it represents a welcome contrast with such contrary values. Just the knowledge of the existence of a place like Glastenbury, an important component of the large, uninhabited, heavily forested, high-elevation spine of the Green Mountains, holds enormous appeal for many. Not everyone would want to live there, but the fact that such a township survives so near to civilization—within a day's drive of cities with millions of people—carries profound value. There is also significance in the realization that all citizens of the U.S. own 96.3 percent of Glastenbury's twenty-seven thousand acres, which are in the Green Mountain National Forest. Actually, they are yours and mine.

Benning Wentworth, the longest serving governor in American colonial history, died in 1770 before he could profit from all his scheming to create towns west of the Connecticut River. He drew lines on a piece of parchment and then hoped to get the resulting towns settled and populated before the New York authorities became too assertive. In Glastenbury, because of the extensive rugged topography, settlement proved next to impossible. If only the duplicitous Benning and his dilatory proprietors could see Glastenbury today—96 percent of it is now National Forest. They created something valuable for the ages.

Side Hill Farm

                              Glastenbury
He mowed those seven acres left now, his pair
with cutter bar pulled through the summer making
a kind of lawn of what was once a field.
The buildings stood, or what was left of them;
a roof, a crib would snap and sag; soon enough
each one would list until it fell. The docks
for loading logs remained, like the hulls of ships
beached on the hillside. Boys to the city gone,
and men to Holden's Mill down hill in town.

No fume of gasoline, but cries of crow
and shape of hawk shadowed vole along
the field he mowed out of a lingering care
for those days, black rotted lumber ramps
behind a scrim of wild cucumber, bush clover.
The owner died and family moved, acres
to corn gone fallow. No reason to hold on,
up here where no one meaning business came,
but maybe on an afternoon picnickers
would hike their way up Glastenbury ledge
to use his field, warm faience-green about
to be buried in long plots of underbrush,
and popples getting started. Woodchucks found it;
hillocks of earth rose at their tunnel doors.

But now they file to hedgerows, lilac and such
where loggers built their little hamlet; dig
in deep. Before the season closes down
they have advanced to take positions in cellars
of houses left to tumble; out from under
they climb to graze; pause there waiting, listening
to the grind and thump when he at twilight back
from work down valley cuts the master's field
rough clumps of grass smoothed out until a trim
lawn comes round again for him; and the budged
woodchucks watch, make do with what's at hand,
munch to roundness, stay on, and do not care.

                              —Stephen Sandy

NOTES

Chapter 1.
Much of the description of Benning Wentworth's aggressive chartering of Vermont towns is based on Clifton K. Shipton's biography of Wentworth in *New England Life in the Eighteenth Century: Representative Biographies from Sibley's Harvard Graduates*, paperback edition, 1995, published by the Belknap Press of Harvard University Press and copyrighted by the Massachusetts Historical Society.

Chapter 2.
A box that contains records of the Glastenbury proprietors is kept in the Special Collections archive in the Bailey-Howe Library at the University of Vermont in Burlington.

Chapter 3.
References to early descriptions of the town of Glastenbury are mostly sourced in the chapter's text. An excellent website is www.vermontcivilwar.org, which gathers information about Civil War descendants.

Chapter 4.
The work of mapmaker William Blodgett is described in articles by Joseph Parks in the *Bennington Banner*, May 15, 1998, and August 19, 2005.

Biographical information about Trenor W. Park is found in June Barrows, "An American Chronicle," fifteen-volume manuscript about the Hall, Park and McCullough families, at the Bennington Museum and Park-McCullough House. Railroad material is largely from newspaper clippings in the Day Papers Collection at the Bennington Museum.

Chapter 5.
Most information about the charcoal industry, as noted in the text, is derived from the studies by archaeologist Victor R. Rolando, and in Rolando's book, *Two Hundred Years of Soot and Sweat: The History and Archeology of Vermont's Iron, Charcoal, and Lime Industries*, published by the Vermont Archaeological Society, 1992.

Chapter 6.
Articles from the *Bennington Reformer* about the death of John Harbour were contributed by Dr. John L. Howard of Edelstein, Illinois, a grandson of the victim. Some accounts of the murder can be found in the *Bennington Banner* as indexed in the Day Papers Collection in the Bennington Museum.

Background on the history of deer season in Vermont comes from a 1964 report by Florence J. Perry, "Progress Report of the Vermont Fish and Game Department: From Colonization and Depredation to Conservation and Education," with help from longtime staffer John Hall.

James H. Livington's biography is found in "Genealogical and Family History of the State of Vermont," compiled by Hiram Carleton and published by Lewis Publishing Co. of New York and Chicago in 1903.

Chapter 7.
Virtually all material in this chapter about the brief flowering of a summer resort can be found in the indexed clippings in the Day Papers Collection at the Bennington Museum.

Chapter 8.
The saga of disincorporation has been assembled from a study of microfilm of newspaper coverage of the time, chiefly the *Rutland Herald, Burlington Free Press* and *Bennington Banner*. Disappearances of Middie Rivers and Paula Welden are based on Bennington and Rutland newspaper accounts and interviews by the author.

Chapter 9.
Details of Trenor Park's involvement with the Panama Railroad can be found in David McCullough's *The Path Between the Seas*, published by Simon & Schuster, 1977.

Biographical data on Rowland Hazard are found in Richard M. Dubiel, "The Road to Fellowship: The Role of the Emmanuel Movement and the Jacoby Club in the Development of Alcoholics Anonymous," Hindsfoot Foundation; from a biography on www.barefootsworld.net; and in the Hazard family papers, held by the Rhode Island Historical Society.

Dr. Richard F. Sterba wrote his own memoir, *Reminiscences of a Viennese Psychoanalyst*, published in 1982 by Wayne State University Press. His daughter, Monika Sterba Schneider, under the pseudonym Frances Oliver, wrote *Girl in a Freudian Slip*, published in 2005 by Perron Press of Great Britain, which contains chapters on the family's many summers in Glastenbury.

Information about Clyde Elwell, "the dog man," comes from his obituary in the *Bennington Banner* May 9, 1958, and public records.

Chapter 10.
The history of National Forest acquisitions was traced from deeds on file at Green Mountain National Forest headquarters in Rutland, Vermont.

Forest Watch of Richmond, Vermont, contributed a statement and several photographs (www.forestwatch.org).

Chapter 11.
Information about zoning in Glastenbury is based on the author's membership and participation in the Bennington Regional Commission and Glastenbury Zoning Board, and on public records.

Chapter 12.
Current municipal information on Glastenbury is from public documents, the town's grand list and tax bills, courtesy of Supervisor Rickey L. Harrington.

BIBLIOGRAPHY

By the nature of the subject—an unorganized town in Vermont—little has been published on Glastenbury, so there are relatively few sources to list. Much of this book is based on the author's own knowledge and experiences as a Vermont citizen, hiker, newspaper editor, journalist, photographer, historian, librarian, selectman, member of a zoning board and a regional planning commission.

Oliver, Frances (Monika Sterba Schneider). *Girl in a Freudian Slip: A Memoir*. Penzance, UK: Perron Press, 2005.

Putnam, Palmer Cosslett. *Power from the Wind*. New York: Van Nostrand Reinhold Co., 1948.

Sherman, Michael, Gene Sessions and P. Jeffrey Potash. *Freedom and Unity: A History of Vermont*. Barre: Vermont Historical Society, 2004. A single-volume history of the state.

Shipton, Clifton K. *New England Life in the Eighteenth Century: Representative Biographies from Sibley's Harvard Graduates*. Cambridge: Belknap Press of Harvard University Press, 1995.

Sterba, Richard F., MD. *Reminiscences of a Viennese Psychoanalyst*. Detroit, MI: Wayne State University Press, 1982.

Swift, Esther Monroe. *Vermont Place-Names: Footprints of History*. Brattleboro, VT: Stephen Greene Press, 1977. This book offers a thumbnail sketch of every town and county in Vermont.

INDEX

A

Allen, Ethan 15, 20, 21
Appalachian Trail 104, 111

B

Beers, F. W. 33, 34, 35, 85
Beethoven, Ludwig von 97
Bennington & Glastenbury 11, 35, 36, 38, 41, 44, 46, 50, 68
Bennington Museum 9, 49, 68, 91, 124, 125
Bennington Regional Commission 14, 114, 125
Blodgett, William 38, 124
Burden, Henry 41
Burlington 22, 78, 81, 82, 83, 106, 124, 125

C

charcoal kilns 11, 14, 36, 46, 118
Child, Hamilton 33
Civil War 35, 36, 46, 96, 124
Connecticut River 16, 17, 18, 19, 122
Crowley, John 54

D

Day, Henry Clay 68, 71, 74
Dearcopp, Charlie 44
deer season 56, 58, 67, 88, 125

E

Elwell, Clyde 99, 125

F

Fay, Benjamin 24
Fayville 11, 24, 35, 54, 77, 80, 98, 104, 117
Fisk, Bill 12
Forest Watch 110, 111, 125
Freud, Sigmund 80, 94, 96, 97, 100
Frost, Robert 5, 117

G

Glastonbury 19, 90
Glazier, Ben 28
Green Mountain Boys 16, 20, 21, 24
Green Mountain Club 51, 111, 113
Green Mountain National Forest 14, 90, 92, 101, 111, 117, 122, 125

H

Harbour, John 53, 56, 58, 59, 60, 61, 62, 64, 65, 67, 68, 88, 124
Harrington, Rickey 9, 14, 87, 122
Harvard 17, 20, 29, 124, 126
Hazard, Rowland 80, 96, 97, 125
Henderson, Jim 9, 14, 122
Hewes 28, 29, 30, 77
Howard, Dr. John R. 9, 56
Howe, Frank E. 58, 84

INDEX

J

Jung, Carl 80, 96

K

Killian, Edgar 93, 95

L

Livingston, James H. 58, 73
Long Trail 11, 12, 50, 51, 88, 102, 104, 105, 110, 111, 117

M

MacIntyre, Barbara 114, 122
Mallory, Chet 113
Matteson 25, 28, 29
Matteson, Peter 25, 26
Mattison 28, 35, 77, 78, 80, 81, 82, 83, 85, 87, 88, 97, 98, 120
McCullough, Hall Park 81, 91, 92, 101, 104
McDonald 28, 29, 30, 35, 54, 77
McDowell, Henry 54
Mitchell, Robert W. 83

N

Nash, C. Howard 110

P

Park, Trenor W. 33, 38, 39, 91, 104, 124
Properties of America 114, 115, 116

R

Revolutionary War 18, 28, 38
Rhode Island 30, 35, 80, 90, 96, 125
Rivers, Middie 88, 125
Robinson, Jonathan 23, 24, 25, 26
Robinson, Moses 23, 25, 26
Robinson, Samuel 19, 20, 22, 23, 25, 26, 29
Robson, David 26, 28
Rolando, Victor 9, 14, 46
Rutland 29, 33, 41, 46, 48, 49, 51, 53, 56, 58, 78, 81, 83, 106, 113, 125

S

Schurink, Henk 98–100
Scott, Robert G. 104, 119, 120

Scott, Trenor 102, 104, 119, 121
Scott, William R. 92, 93, 101
Searsburg 40, 44, 77, 82, 84, 113
Serkin, Rudolph 99
Somerset 12, 19, 21, 23, 30, 32, 36, 38, 40, 41, 51, 77, 78, 81, 82, 83, 84, 85, 95, 102, 105, 106
Sterba, Dr. Editha 97–99, 114
Sterba, Dr. Richard 80, 94, 97, 100

T

Taylor, Katie 78, 81, 83
Thacher, Ebby 96

V

Vermont Archaeology Society 46
Viereck, Phillip 93, 95

W

Welden, Paula 88, 89, 125
Wentworth, Benning 15, 16, 17, 19, 20, 22, 27, 106, 122, 124
Wilderness 14, 15, 107, 108, 110, 111
Williams, Samuel 29
Wilson, Bill 96
Wolter, Carlo 44
Woodford 11, 12, 18, 22, 23, 26, 32, 34, 35, 36, 40, 41, 44, 46, 49, 50, 51, 52, 56, 58, 60, 63, 70, 72, 73, 75, 76, 88, 91, 95, 101, 102, 111, 117

Y

Yale 30, 96
Yoder, Charles 14, 119

www.ingramcontent.com/pod-product-compliance
Lightning Source LLC
Chambersburg PA
CBHW060809100426
42813CB00004B/1001